THE
SELF-CONFIDENT
CHILD

THE
SELF-CONFIDENT
CHILD

JEAN YODER, M.D.
and
WILLIAM PROCTOR

Facts On File Publications
New York, New York • Oxford, England

The Self-Confident Child

Copyright © 1988 by Jean Yoder and William Proctor

LIBRARY OF CONGRESS
Library of Congress Cataloging-in-Publication Data

Yoder, Jean.
    The self-confident child / by Jean Yoder and William Proctor.
      p.   cm.
    Includes index.
    ISBN 0-8160-1270-9 : $22.95 (est.)
    1. Child rearing. 2. Self-confidence. 3. Child development.
  I. Proctor, William. II. Title.
  HQ769.Y555   1988
  649'.1—dc 19

British CIP data available on request

Printed in the United States of America

10 9 8 7 6 5 4 3 2 1

Contents

Preface

In the years that I've spent working with children and parents in my medical practice—as well as in my own experience as a parent—I've discovered that one of the most important qualities for a child's future happiness and success is self-confidence. Yet despite the essential role that this trait plays in a child's development, most books and articles on parenting only touch upon the subject. Too often, they fail to deal directly with such key questions as:

- What is self-confidence?
- Why is it such an important quality for children?
- What steps can parents take to give this all-important characteristic to their youngsters?

In the following pages, I've drawn heavily on my own work as a pediatrician, as well as on the scientific and popular literature, to describe what self-confidence is. Also, I've tried to show how you, as a parent, can help your child acquire this trait. The case studies and examples have been masked to prevent the identification of the individuals involved. Also, we have alternated the use of feminine and masculine pronouns in the text—just to make clear that the points we are making apply to *both* girls and boys!

As we've worked on this topic, my coauthor Bill Proctor and I have frequently found ourselves consulting our spouses and examining our own relationships with our children. As a result, we've gained an intensely personal perspective on how this powerful quality of self-confidence can make a major difference in one's life. So for helping to keep us "honest" and completely down to earth in our presentation, I want to thank my husband, Joe, and my two children, Bonnie and Keith; and Bill wants to express his gratitude to his wife, Pam, and their son, Michael.

Also, we're very grateful for the editorial and research assistance provided by Kim Flowers, Fafa Demasio and Henry Lee.

Finally, it's our fervent hope that the explanations and advice you'll find in this book will assist you in teaching your own child how to become more poised, self-assured and, indeed, self-confident—as he or she moves toward adulthood.

Jean Yoder, M.D.

THE
SELF-CONFIDENT
CHILD

PART ONE

An Introduction to Self-Confidence During Childhood

1

The Ultimate Gift

If you're like most parents, there's no question you'd do practically anything for your child: move mountains, fend off wild beasts, attend Suzuki violin classes. No sacrifice is too great when the future of that young son or daughter seems at stake.

In short, you want junior to have the best of everything—right? That usually means possessing high aspirations and goals . . . solid and supportive friends . . . an ability to lead others . . . an inquiring and creative mind, honed razor sharp by a good education . . . a stimulating and meaningful occupation . . . a happy marriage and family life . . . a fine set of personal values.

And that's just the beginning.

Now, I know that many nonparents (and also some *seasoned* parents) may write off this list of achievements and qualities as an advanced case of wishful thinking—but not the new or perennially optimistic mother or father. We live in an era when "superparents" are trying to push toddlers and even infants to become "superbabies"—kids who are supposedly on the fast track to Olympic medals, Ivy-League educations and corporate presidencies, even before they enter first grade.

This frenetic, high-pressure approach to child rearing is doomed from the start for one simple reason: It completely misses the point of effective child rearing. It's designed to endow a youngster with superior *outward* skills that are supposed to ensure success, but what that youngster really needs is a reservoir of *inner* strength and moral fiber.

In other words, it's a classic case of putting the cart before the horse. In my years as a pediatrician and counselor to parents, I've discovered that when parents concentrate on building up the inner child, the outward abilities and achievements naturally follow. But the reverse tends not to occur.

So, what is the exact nature of this inner strength that can enhance your child's future, and how can you help your youngster develop it?

Specifically, there's a personal trait you can encourage in your child, one which leads naturally to outstanding achievement and many fine qualities. It's a parent's *ultimate gift* to a child—the gift of self-confidence.

In brief, self-confidence is the active, effective expression of inner feelings of self-worth, self-esteem and self-understanding. The child who is self-confident has the ability to

- be assertive, without being overly aggressive
- stick to his beliefs, even when everyone else is standing against him
- make new friends easily
- stick with a job until it's completed—and be secure enough to know that his best is good enough
- take defeats and rejections in stride—and bounce back quickly and energetically
- work well with others as a "team" player
- assume a leadership role without hesitation when appropriate and
- *expect* to become a leader, at least on some occasions.

Moreover, self-confidence has a "ripple" effect. That is, if your child is self-confident, he'll be more likely to acquire many other great qualities as well. For example, he'll probably "make" his own luck, handle stress well, exercise better judgment, perform better in school and sports and become about as popular as he wants to be.

At its essence, self-confidence is an *action*-oriented quality. The level of a child's self-confidence determines to a large degree how well she performs with others; what personal goals she sets and is able to achieve; and the effectiveness with which she handles life's problems.

Without self-confidence a youngster is severely limited in what he can accomplish. Also—and perhaps most important of all—he can't enjoy fully those objectives he does achieve.

But *with* self-confidence, he'll look forward to the next challenge with an inner assurance. Finally, true self-confidence will not only lead a child toward achievement; it will also pave the way to greater happiness and contentment in life. If a person develops self-confidence as a child, he will have greater potential for success and happiness as an adult.

So, that, in a nutshell, is what self-confidence is all about. Now, what are the chances that your child can get a healthy dose of it?

My basic message in this book is very simple and, I hope, reassuring to anxious parents: *You* possess the power to instill this essential quality of self-confidence in your sons and daughters. It's a matter of learning to teach your youngster how to become more assured and effective.

Unfortunately, however, many forces are at work to undercut the development of self-confidence in children. Consider just a few that I've noticed in recent years:

- Textbooks on child development often ignore this key quality and so specialists who advise parents tend to overlook it, too. To be sure, there are innumerable studies on ''self-esteem'' and ''self-worth,'' but these reports don't bridge the gap between ideas and action. They don't tell you *how* you can help your child develop these inner strengths.
- There has been a significant increase in the number of working mothers in recent years. As a result, today there are more than five million ''latchkey children'' who, during some part of each day, must fend for themselves.

  These youngsters often lack the support systems of self-confidence that are so essential to the nurturing of this quality. In a number of cases, these kids have to reach deep inside their own little beings and try to muster the courage to enter an empty home or apartment by themselves. They may also have to conquer a sense of personal rejection that stems from a feeling that no one cares enough to meet them.

  This is not always the case, of course. There *are* latchkey children who develop plenty of self-confidence. Perhaps they just naturally have the tough inner fiber that's required to overcome the absence of a strong parental presence. But far too many of the latchkey kids are classic examples of how a person can become independent without at the same time becoming self-confident.

- Back in 1960, when parents tended to be around their kids more often, the suicide rate in the 15-to-24 age category was 5.2 per 100,000. Nearly three decades later, it has soared almost threefold to 13 per 100,000. This horrendous development has coincided with a decline in the quality and stability of family life. Ironically, the children who choose to kill themselves are often the very ones who are quite popular and have achieved great things at school. In other words, they have "success" without self-esteem.

- The shocking increase in divorce, desertion and illegitimacy has resulted in hundreds of thousands of single-parent homes in our society. The Foundation for Child Development, in a four-year study of kids in New York City, found that one in every three children lives in a family headed only by a mother. Also, in less than a decade over a quarter of a million children have been born to unmarried women.

"What happens to the children of New York City is indicative of the experience of children around the nation," the foundation reported ominously.

It doesn't require a degree in education or child psychology to appreciate the fact that such children desperately need more assurance and support from adults. They need a big, healthy dose of self-confidence; the lack of it can have tragic results.

So, what can you as a parent do to give your child this great gift of self-confidence?

The answer to this question lies first in understanding the very special relationship between parent and infant. Up until the 1970s, much of the professional literature assumed that the baby was a passive part of the environment. In fact, it wasn't that long ago that certain authorities actually believed babies were blind and deaf!

Today, we know that the one-to-one, interpersonal contact between the parent and the child forms an indispensable basis for self-esteem and self-confidence. In fact, this close contact is essential for practically all achievement and happiness later in life. This relationship, which becomes especially important during the first six months of life, is what might be called a "relationship of reciprocity." That is, it's a two-way interaction, with contact often being initiated by the infant.

The responses of the adult are critical. They form the baby's earliest experience of the environment as a predictable, stable, dependable place. These first interactions also form the platform for his slowly developing core of self-confidence. Another way of putting this is that children must first develop what might be called "other-confidence" through predictable patterns of interaction with their parents, and especially with the mother. This "other-confidence" will later evolve into an internalized *self*-confidence and will also be echoed in adult life in the trust they are able to put in other human beings and even in God.

Disaster can result if the responses of the caretaker to the child are inadequate during the very early years. For example, by the very nature of the hospital system, infants who are born prematurely and have to stay in an institution for long periods lack the close nurturing relationship that a mother can provide. Hospitals enforce rigorous schedules for feeding and other basic services for infants. But in general, they can't be responsive to the *individual* needs and demands of a child. Meals at four-hour intervals, for instance, may not always come at the time that the youngster is really hungry.

As a matter of fact, some of these unfortunate babes can't even survive without a fundamental experience of personal responsiveness in their world. Yes, melodramatic as it may sound, infants can actually die for lack of human contact. They may be well fed; they may be clean. But their spirits and psyches lack proper nurture, and they just seem to wither away. Hospitals are increasingly recognizing this danger as they add visiting hours and alter staff schedules so as to "humanize" care of infants.

Even if a child's life isn't in jeopardy, multiple "surrogate mothers" who care for one child, such as a series of nurses in a hospital, may by their sheer numbers dangerously undermine his self-confidence. And there's a fairly simple explanation. Inevitably, each caretaker, even with the best of intentions, reacts differently to the same child's behavior. Thus, with each new parent substitute, the child must start all over again in her effort to get adult signals straight.

The result: The world becomes less predictable, less constant, less controllable. Sometimes, during the child's struggle to manage more than one or two persons, the challenge may become overwhelming, and he may finally give up. Incapable of trying to figure out how to handle a succession of caretakers, the infant withdraws. He becomes more or less detached from his environment. In extreme cases, he may not even signal very strongly when he is hungry or tired.

In short, these babies, damaged by the unresponsiveness or unpredictability of their world, exhibit at the tenderest ages the ravages of a lack of self-confidence. They simply don't think they have the capacity to cope with life at all.

For that matter, even short-term hospital stays can have a devastating impact on a child's emotional environment. The array of problems that may arise are cataloged in excellent detail in the book *Psychosocial Research on Pediatric Hospitalization and Health Care* (1985), edited by Dr. Richard H. Thompson, director of the Child Life and Family Education Department at the University of Chicago. The contributors to this book cite a wide range of studies conducted since 1965 on problems that accompany hospital stays by children, even those that last for only a week or two. Apparently, according to these experts, the two periods when children are most vulnerable to the negative impact of hospitalizations are early childhood, including the preschool years, and adolescence.

After such stays, adolescents tend to develop a higher incidence of behavior problems in classrooms, trouble with reading skills, detentions for delinquency and unstable job patterns. Younger children who have been hospitalized tend to develop greater fear of strangers, castration concerns, lower self-esteem and a greater dependency.

What these studies are saying is quite clear: There is no substitute for a parental presence. Most of the children who exhibited these negative reactions to hospitalization had been uprooted from their normal family environment completely, with little or no efforts made to provide a continuity between the home and the hospital. Yet the negative effects of this kind of change of environment can be minimized if parents and nurses will just take a few simple steps to cushion the blow of hospitalization. These include:

- more parental involvement in the hospital, including an effort by parents to stay with their children as much as possible during this period away from home
- arrangements by parents to sleep in the same room with the child in the hospital and
- "primary nursing" care, in which one nurse is assigned to a particular child for much of the day.

I've also seen withdrawal in infants who have been hospitalized for long periods. It's truly a frightening spectacle; but it's not irreversible. If the mother stays with her baby in the hospital or assumes a regular, predictable, major role in his care, he can gradually become a noisy, normal child again. One sign of the return of emotional health is when he starts signaling loudly his discomfort over hunger or soiled diapers.

Of course, hospitals aren't the only potential in undetermining self-confidence in a child. I have similar reservations about daily child care or preschool programs that lack the flexibility to allow young children to rest when they are tired, or to play when they are restless. Because such flexibility can't be built into every program, it may be advisable to include "days off" each week. This allows a child to get in touch again with his own natural schedules.

My own three-year-old loves her school two mornings a week. But at the same time, she looks forward to extra sleep and quiet mornings at home on alternate days. The rigidity of the nine-to-five, five-day work week comes too soon as it is! Why impose it on a child before she's ready?

So for me, the evidence is overwhelming that attentive parenthood is indispensable to the blossoming of infant self-confidence. The mother and father should learn to recognize, understand and be responsive to their child's emotional needs, even in infancy.

The best way to gain this knowledge is to observe your youngster closely and sensitize yourself to your baby's special personality traits and responses. Try to understand what a certain grimace conveys; what different kinds of cries reflect about the child's comfort levels; and what emotions are coming across in various cackles and "baby talk." Then, as you come to understand the uniqueness of your youngster, you can take active steps to shape and direct that malleable infant into a competent, secure, self-assured personality.

Of course, all this requires a lot of close parental contact with a child; it can't be done very effectively through babysitters or surrogates. To help you achieve the necessary level of personal involvement, here are four key strategies which I enthusiastically endorse for any parent who hopes to encourage the maximum self-confidence in a son or daughter. These strategies, summarized here, represent themes which will run through the entire book.

STRATEGY #1: MOTHERS, MAKE A COMMITMENT!

Every young child needs extensive exposure to its own mother. You *must* spend time to get to know your own unique child. We all come into parenting with preconceived notions and expectations. Sometimes, it takes years to discover who this new person is and what he can and wants to do.

So I recommend that for at least the first three years of her baby's life, and preferably for the first five, the mother should give up or subordinate her outside career. I know this may be an unpopular suggestion to some people. It may not even be possible for those families hard-pressed by economic problems. But believe me, once the necessities of food, clothing and shelter are met, you and your time are the most important things you can provide for your child. So if you can leave work during those early years—or at least cut back on the amount of time you're spending on the job—you can expect your child to reap significant rewards in later years.

In my own case, I worked until my first child, my daughter Bonnie, was 18 months old. During that 18 months, I placed her with another mother, a kind of "nanny" who was looking after her own child at the same time that she was taking care of Bonnie. During the day, Bonnie stayed with this woman at an apartment that was near my office, and so I could pop in periodically or at least be available on short notice if I was needed.

But then, I decided that even though it would be something of a financial hardship, I really should devote all of my time to Bonnie and also to our next child, Keith, who by then was very much a part of our plans. I'll be quite frank with you: It wasn't easy to make the decision to leave a thriving medical practice and concentrate full time on child rearing. But I really felt, after my own studies and observations in this area, that for the first four to five years of their lives, my children had to be a priority for me. In my case, that meant suspending my career and staying home with them.

I don't want to be rigid about any of these suggestions: I realize that many mothers simply can't leave work and devote full time to their children during these early years. Certainly, you needn't feel guilty about what you simply can't do, and, in fact, many children go on to lead happy, healthy lives, even if they don't have a full-time mother on hand during their formative years.

At the same time, I think we should all recognize what a weighty responsibility child rearing is and how decisive the primary caretaker can be in fostering the development of a solid sense of self-esteem and self-confidence. If you find that there's no way you can devote all your time during the early years of your child's life to his or her upbringing, then you should at least be *extremely* careful about the individual you choose to do the job for you. The decision about getting a nanny, governess or babysitter for your youngster is at least as important as any career decision or other personal step that you'll ever take.

But what about the father? Up to this point, I've emphasized the responsibility of the mother as the primary caretaker for the child. But these days, the role of the father has assumed increasing importance and received considerable publicity.

To be sure, mothers continue to be more involved in taking the lead in child rearing than fathers. For example, by 1985, 23 percent of the 62.5 million children in the United States under the age of 18 lived in single-parent families, according to the federal Census Bureau. And in 90 percent of those single-parent homes, the parent was the mother. And even in two-parent families, fathers tend to leave the main burden of child care to the mother, according to research done by Ross D. Parke, professor of psychology at the University of Illinois at Champaign-Urbana.

In a classic 1972 study, Parke and his associates spent a great deal of time in a hospital maternity ward in Madison, Wisconsin, observing interactions between parents of newborn babies. In general, they discovered that fathers and mothers related about the same way to their children in terms of touching, talking and otherwise showing affection.

Parke concluded that fathers were as competent in dealing with their infants as the mothers and that the men seemed to have as much potential to be good caretakers as the mothers. At the same time, however, Parke found that the fathers usually let the mothers take care of the children when both parents were present.

Other research has shown that fathers tend to be selective in the children to whom they relate best. Douglas Sawin of the University of Texas, in collaboration with Parke, has found that fathers are more inclined to get involved in touching and talking to firstborn sons than to daughters or to children who were born later in the sibling order.

Ongoing research is being conducted in the area of fatherhood by such experts as Dr. James A. Levine, formerly with Wellesley College and later the director of the Fatherhood Project of the Bank Street College of Education in Manhattan. This research effort, which has been funded by the Ford Foundation, the Rockefeller Family Fund and the Levi Strauss Foundation, has focused on such issues as paternity leave, custody mediation services for separated parents and other involvement by fathers in parenting.

As research continues in this ground-breaking area of contemporary fatherhood, the questions naturally arise, "Where is parenthood heading in our culture? Are we on the verge of an explosion of increased involvement of fathers in parenting?"

Probably, we won't see a tremendous shift in child care, with huge numbers of fathers taking over responsibilities from mothers. Even researchers who are on the cutting edge in this field are quite cautious. Dr. Michael E. Lamb, a professor of psychology, psychiatry and pediatrics at the University of Utah and also codirector of the Fatherhood Project, puts it this way: "I think we need to underscore that in this research and in our other work, the Project is not plugging father involvement. We're not saying it should be a goal for all fathers. But for those who may want greater involvement, what are the barriers to their participation?" (*The New York Times*, December 7, 1981)

Much of the current research is focusing on "total family interaction, the family systems perspective," Dr. Levine says. In other words, the experts are exploring ways that fathers can participate more in the upbringing of their children without necessarily completely supplanting the traditional role of the mother. In fact, most findings indicate that *both* parents are absolutely essential to the healthy emotional and social development of a child. Dr. T. Berry Brazelton, director of the Child Development Unit of Children's Hospital Medical Center in Boston, has made these observations: "Mother has more of a tendency to teach the baby about inner control . . . . the father adds a different dimension, a sort of play dimension, an excitement dimension, teaching the baby another very important thing—how to get *back* in control." (*New York Times Magazine*, June 17, 1979, 52)

In short, then, mothers and fathers have different but essential roles in child rearing. To be sure, in most cases, it's the mother who will take the lead in this important area of family life. Still, I'll be assuming throughout this book that *both* parents should be involved in helping build up a youngster's self-confidence throughout childhood.

STRATEGY #2: FORMULATE A SELF-CONFIDENCE PLAN

The parents must develop a concrete, detailed plan to develop their child's self-confidence. Then, they must be willing to put that plan into effect and enforce it.

Of course, any plan that is going to be relevant to a child's real needs has to be based on firsthand observation. So, the close contact of the mother and child in Strategy #1 is an important precondition for Strategy #2. That is, the parent or parents, who are by definition in close contact with the child, must first understand the personality of the youngster. Then, they should list *on paper* the key things they want to do to generate self-confidence in their child.

It's extremely important for the parents to establish solid, open lines of communication between themselves as they formulate the basic self-confidence plan for their child. To this end, writing things down can be quite helpful. That way, each parent will be more likely to understand precisely what the other has in mind.

The specific steps and goals that should make up your personal self-confidence plan will become clearer as you get further into this book. But for now, keep this important principle in mind: Every self-confidence plan requires discipline if it's going to work properly. "Spare the rod and spoil the child" may not exactly express the child-rearing ideal these days. But undirected early development, characterized by the valueless permissiveness of current society, will only result in a lack of identity and self-assurance for your youngster.

STRATEGY #3: LET YOUR CHILD'S MIND AND EMOTIONS DEVELOP AT THEIR OWN PACE.

This seems like such a reasonable, obvious idea, doesn't it? But too often, in their anxiety to turn their kids into high achievers, parents forget.

It's true, of course, that there is a series of "life steps" or developmental phases in the evolution of the thinking and emotional development of all children. But there are no hard-and-fast cut-off points by which any particular child is supposed to walk, talk, eat with table utensils or parrot back the alphabet. The child development expert Jean Piaget says that the developmental ages of a child are "average and approximate," and that's a key point to remember. There are no precise times when your child is supposed to be doing this or that.

Even as we acknowledge the validity of this principle of broad developmental phases, with fuzzy beginning and ending points, I know it's hard not to worry about how your child is doing. But try to put things in perspective. There's no formula for knowing exactly where your child should be in her development at a given age. A complex set of factors, including inherited tendencies and environment, determines the way a child passes through the various stages of development. Trying to push your youngster in a way that is inconsistent with his own developmental clock is not only futile but may even be damaging. One reason is that this approach sets the child up for failure.

One example of such damage came to my attention recently when a young mother approached me for help. She had enrolled her son when he was only five months old in various classes that were supposed to enhance his ability to deal with numbers, language concepts and motor skills. By the age of 14 months, she was announcing proudly to neighbors that he had learned to climb stairs. Moreover, she was convinced he was well on his way to still loftier achievements.

Sadly, however, even as this mother was spending most of her time chauffeuring her son to one "better baby" class after another, she was *depriving* him of wholesome interaction with her. Playing with Mommy would have been infinitely more rewarding to both of them than the "pressure-the-child" programs he had been attending.

And that isn't the worst of it. As the boy progressed toward his third birthday, he began to rebel actively and to lose several of his new skills. To make matters even more difficult, the mother unexpectedly became pregnant. Now, she lacked the energy to cart him around to his superbaby classes. When the new baby arrived, she felt even more fatigued. Yet she had put herself in a bind: She feared that if she pulled the older son out of some of his special activities, she would be giving up prematurely and might do him irreparable harm.

Finally, this mother reached the end of her rope. Exhausted, she decided she simply couldn't deal with two active children in the way she had been attempting. So she decided to take a rest from mothering. She placed her older son in a day-care center during the morning five days a week. Also, she took him out of most of his special classes, except for one or two that he himself selected. As a result of the day-care help and also her decision to decrease the pressure on her son and herself, she has recouped much of her energy and seems to be doing quite well.

I'm not so sure about the child. He is, to put it mildly, overanxious about things. Also, he's obsessed with trying to please his mother.

The constant pressure on the boy apparently made him nervous almost from infancy about performing properly for his mother. Then, her sudden withdrawal from his presence when he had just turned three, along with the appearance of a younger sibling, totally disrupted any security he may have gleaned from his environment. His actions reflect a classic failure of a child to develop self-confidence.

But the mother is helping to turn the tide, I think. She is restoring a normal environment and showering him with love and reassurance. Also, she now always emphasizes the positive: She doesn't criticize him for "accidents." And when he does spill something or break a glass, she explains that there's nothing wrong with that: All they have to do is just clean it up!

Such a case history indicates what can happen to a young mother whose attachment to her firstborn progresses from normal love to an obsession with perfection. When a parent begins to drive and push a child outside his or her normal channels of development, there's going to be trouble.

So, the essence of this third strategy for developing self-confidence is, relax enough to stay *flexible*. Certainly, it's important to have a plan for your child's development. But that plan must always be adjusted to the special traits that make your child an individual. In short, he's a person different from anyone else who has ever been, or ever will be, born into this world.

The roots of almost any adult's self-confidence can usually be traced to an early appreciation by the parents of the youngster's individuality. The wisest parents know that no two children will follow one timetable in their early development. There will be some general similarities, but peculiar traits and differences will be more the rule than the exception. Even identical twins won't pursue exactly the same activities or come up with precisely the same life scenarios.

As early in life as the first few weeks of infancy, there are distinct differences. There may be major variations in activity levels, in feeding demands, in sleep patterns and in the times of the day when there is the greatest alertness. Yes, there are "early birds" and "night owls" among the youngest babies, just as there are among mature adults!

Because diverse factors have to be taken into account as you begin to build your child's self-confidence, the process can get rather complex. You can't rely on every technique you used with your first child to imbue your second with self-assurance. Yet, as unpredictable as such differences can make life, there's something really wonderful about this uniqueness. It makes life more exciting and injects an element of wonder that wouldn't be possible otherwise.

STRATEGY #4: HELP YOUR YOUNGSTER DEVELOP A "TEAM TEMPERAMENT"

Even though a recognition of your child's individuality is extremely important, there's another side to that coin. One of the major ingredients I've noticed in the self-confident child—and it's also a quality which characterizes most self-confident adults—is the ability to mix and work well with peers. This is what I call a "team temperament." Much of what follows in this book is directed toward helping the parent shape and enhance this trait.

The extreme individualist, such as the loner who shuns joint enterprises with his playmates, is far less likely to achieve success, assurance and satisfaction in maturity. I'm reminded of the case of one very bright boy who always scored near the top on standardized tests that measure intelligence. He was also a good student and graduated high in his class in prep school.

But then, when he entered a fine, top-ranked university, his life began to come apart. He had experienced a close relationship with his mother, and so the framework had been present for the development of a solid core of self-confidence. But, unfortunately, his mother had used their hours together to encourage him to be too dependent on her. Also, she had discouraged him from developing a broad range of friendships.

As a result, he possessed a great deal of "book learning," but his social growth had been completely stunted. He had never learned to play and work with other kids. So when he was off on his own in college, he couldn't handle the tensions and challenges of dealing with roommates and other peers without his mother's help. He was a very unhappy young man during those years and found himself becoming more and more isolated.

The situation got even worse when he contemplated the choice of careers at the end of his college experience. He was drawn to the business world, and that presented some problems. To succeed and find happiness in most jobs, it's often as important to get along with others as it is to do an expert job. In business, there is an especially high premium on working with peers and impressing superiors.

But this young man lacked the necessary "team temperament." He had no confidence that he could enter into a project with other workers and by charm or force of personality influence them to see things his way. As a result he found himself at a serious disadvantage because he was considered "too distant" or even "antisocial" by his bosses and fellow workers.

Even in those fields where individual talent or solitary achievement are highly valued, such as in the arts or literature, success often depends on working with—or at least influencing—other people. There are exceptions, of course, such as the mad artist or reclusive writer who disdains most human contact and still makes it big. Here, we are talking about the rare and exceptional person who is driven or obsessed. But self-confidence as we are considering it would probably *still* make life more enjoyable or satisfying. Sometimes, these folks have "dropped out" precisely because no one else believed in them. In general, then, no would-be Thoreaus need apply to the Self-Confidence Hall of Fame!

Now, with some of these general strategies in mind, let's move on to the heart of the matter, to the practical techniques that will allow you to bestow the great gift of self-confidence upon your child. First of all, there are five "self-confidence crises" that all children seem to face in their movement toward maturity. The parent who understands what these challenges entail will be in a better position to respond effectively as his child moves through the growing-up process.

2

Confronting the Five Self-Confidence Crises

A decade or two ago, a great many popular writers and academic researchers on child rearing let us down badly.

In their misty-eyed enthusiasm for permissive raising of children, many of them promoted the theory that the child was coequal with the parent. As a result, it was inappropriate, so the argument went, for the adult to assume the role of disciplinarian. The child was supposed to understand very early the foibles and weaknesses of the adult. Then, the very young and the old would "grow together" through the childhood experience.

An endearing, but ridiculous, conceit!

Much of the riotous behavior in our schools—including the petty misbehavior and not-so-petty criminal offenses among our teenagers—can be laid squarely at the door of such permissiveness.

But in the last decade, things have changed. It's become apparent that simply allowing a child to develop "naturally" into adulthood is not enough. Some guidance and planning on the part of the parent are absolutely essential. So there has been a shift in emphasis among the experts: From merely observing the child's growth and allowing it to proceed haphazardly, we have moved toward helping the parent shape the child's destiny. In short, permissiveness has given way to firm direction of the child's personality and future. And a key focus, as we give more direction to our children, must be on the development of that all-important foundational trait, self-confidence.

In my own professional medical work with children and also in my personal experience as a parent, I've identified five milestones in child development that I believe are crucial to the nurturing of a child's self-confidence. These points, which I call the "Five Self-Confidence Crises," are based in part on the work of Melvin Lewis of Yale and also of the great Eric Erikson, with his path-breaking article, "Identity and the Life Cycle." But also, they are derived from my own observations, as I've tried to formulate a practical approach to developing self-confidence in children.

First, let me introduce you briefly to these five crises; then, we'll spend more time on them in later chapters.

CONFIDENCE CRISIS #1:
THE BASIC TRUST CRISIS

During the first few months of life, your youngster isn't aware that he's "different" from his environment or from those people with whom he has most frequent contact. His mother and father are merely extensions of himself. At this stage, your little one is supremely important in his own eyes.

As he gets a little older, say five or six months, he begins to realize that there's a world out there that is distinct from his own tiny being. During this first phase of life, as the child begins to separate himself from outside reality, it's extremely important that the parents maintain an atmosphere of security and trust. There should be a gentle transition from the ultimate nurturing atmosphere of the womb to the hard knocks of the real world.

Because the supportive presence of a parent is essential in this phase, it's important to structure your child's day to encourage considerable warmth and security. Among other things, this means engaging in activities that allow you to be in close physical touch with him. I'm particularly enthusiastic about reading to children—even if your child is at such a tender age that she hasn't yet mastered basic sounds like "goo" or "mama." In fact, this is really reading *with* a child instead of just *to* her, as she turns pages forward and back, points out pictures, snuggles into your lap. The written story here is *not* the main message.

John Rosemond, a prominent psychologist and columnist, reported that one reader asked how soon it was advisable to begin reading to their seven-month-old. Rosemond's answer: "Last month."

He advocates reading to a child at least by six months of age, and preferably younger because, he says, "The nurturing that takes place when a parent reads to a child helps strengthen the child's sense of security." That in turn enhances the youngster's later independence.

Now, I doubt personally that reading per se has much impact on the intellectual development of six-month-old babies. But the attention the child receives during a reading session can't help but bolster his nascent sense of security, and hence his self-confidence. That's what this first stage of developing inner assurance is all about: You want to help the youngster sense a continuity of security between the warmth of the womb and the reliability of his outside environment.

CONFIDENCE CRISIS #2: THE TRAUMATIC TRANSITION FROM INFANCY TO TODDLERHOOD

During this phase, the child is making the nerve-racking transition from "baby" to "big boy" or "big girl." This is a time of independence and autonomy, and the way is also thrown wide open for the child to experience shame and doubt.

The independence comes as your youngster starts learning to walk. As one authority has put it, the beginning of mobility "changes the child's whole perspective on his world."

But with the new independence also comes the possibility of mistakes and failure. So, as that toddler begins to get into mischief around the house, he may also get hurt: He toddles too quickly on a wet deck, slips and falls, and perhaps suffers a serious cut on the lip. That may mean a quick trip to the doctor's office or an emergency room. The experience will also serve as a painful reminder that independence is not without its dangers and difficulties.

Also during this period, which runs into the third year of life, your youngster will begin to struggle for control over his own body. In particular, the problems of toilet training can add plenty of spice to family life.

It's common for children in this phase to want to get off by themselves when they're having a bowel movement. It almost seems as though they know this is not the sort of thing that one does in public. Ironically, adult concern over where, when and how often conflicts with parental beliefs about and the child's need for privacy.

As a child begins to try to gain complete control over bathroom activities with toilet training, there are going to be plenty of accidents and failures that may introduce a large dose of shame, doubt and confusion. On the other hand, when he succeeds, his mastery of potty-training will be perhaps the first major thing in the world that he feels he has really controlled—and he'll be justly proud, especially if his relieved parents can refrain from taking all the credit!

Perhaps the greatest threat to the child's sense of security and well-being during this second confidence crisis will focus on his continuing separation from his mother or primary caretaker. He sees more clearly that most of the world and reality exists apart from him. The child finally sees that there are major limitations between his body and consciousness and the outside environment—an environment which seems increasingly confusing and fractured the more independence he gains.

It's little wonder, then, that youngsters in this transition phase to toddlerhood often begin to act up and throw tantrums. These times are aptly described as the "terrible twos" and the reaction is certainly understandable: There's a crushing weight of responsibility on these tiny shoulders as the separation from mother moves inexorably to its climax.

CONFIDENCE CRISIS #3:
THE SIBLING SALVOS

Just before reaching school age, at about four or five years, many children come face to face with this third major confidence crisis—the limitations that arise from being one of a *group* of children in a family.

A key factor in this phase is learning that the world doesn't revolve around you. There are other kids who have a right to demand a piece of the parents' attention and allegience.

Some of the big questions that pop up are: Does Mommy love me as much as she does Johnny? Why doesn't Daddy have more time to play with me? That wasn't my fault—Mommy is treating me unfairly! Why can Johnny do that, and I can't?

These experiences are particularly critical to a child's later development of self-confidence because they come at a time just before or at the beginning of school, when the youngster meets serious challenges by outsiders.

Also during this phase, your youngster has to learn the difference between what he *can* do and what he *may* do. He learns—reluctantly and often unhappily—the limitations that are intrinsic to him and his talents and abilities. The limitations set by society and reflected in the attitudes of his parents come crashing down on him. And as he begins to make comparisons of his own importance and worth with those of his siblings, he may sense that he's getting the short end of the stick.

It's crucial at this point for parents to focus on being even-handed with all the children. Yet it's also important to give special attention and favor to each individual child, whenever that's possible or necessary.

CONFIDENCE CRISIS #4:
THE CRISIS OF PEER COMPETITION

During the early school years, from about age five or six to puberty, the relationships of a child with his peers grow steadily more important. Competition with friends and classmates comes to the fore. Most commonly, it's expressed as children vie for the favor and attention of the adults in the child's life. The adult in question may be a parent; he may be a teacher; or she may even be a neighbor or casual acquaintance.

Recently, a group of seven-to-nine-year-olds in our neighborhood were waiting for the school bus. As I watched, they got embroiled in an animated discussion about some item that one of the children was holding. It seemed that one little girl had found a printed joke on a package of bubble gum, and they all were laughing at how funny it was. But at the same time, they needed some reinforcement.

So the little girl who had introduced the gum to the group brought the joke over to me. She was obviously hoping desperately that it would make me laugh. Frankly, the joke wasn't very funny, but I laughed anyhow just to make her happy—and indeed, her eyes lit up like little flashlights.

This first encounter set the stage for a parade of children who came to my steps in the hope of getting the same sort of attention and assurance that I had given the first girl. They all walked up to tell me the same joke and waited expectantly to see me laugh. Of course, they all knew that I had heard the story. But it was important for them to get adult reinforcement that they could repeat the joke effectively and provoke a response.

Undoubtedly, many of these children had tried a similar approach with their parents and teachers. And I'm sure that sometimes the response they got was precisely the opposite: "Don't be silly!"

All parents and teachers react that way at one time or another. But it's a real put-down—and can crush a child's self-confidence. For that matter, it doesn't do much for an adult's self-confidence either! After all, what grown-up *really* means it when he says, "Stop me if you've heard this one!"

During the period covered by this fourth confidence crisis, children learn to work hard and be aggressive with one major goal in mind: To raise themselves to a status that is equal to or higher than that of their peers. They all have had enough experience with ridicule and rejection to know that there's a possibility that they may be in some way inferior to others. So a successful interaction with their classmates and friends—and the recognition of their success by important adults—is a typical way to bolster their emerging self-confidence during these early years.

CONFIDENCE CRISIS #5:
THE WARS OF INDEPENDENCE

Finally, in the preadolescent through the teen years, when the older child is fighting to stand on his own two feet and discover who he really is, he confronts the crisis of identity. He asks: Who am I? What am I going to achieve in life? Am I a good enough person to cause other people to respect me? Will someone of the opposite sex ever really love me?

I've called this period the "wars for independence" because it's a time when exasperated parents often bear the brunt of the internal changes and wing-stretchings that go on in their teenagers. This is the period of the old-fashioned "teenage rebellion"—the rebel without a cause that actor James Dean epitomized in the classic film of the same title.

I still recall vividly the experience of one young man who was deeply influenced by the Dean image. He wore his hair like Dean, affected the same pouting and sulking countenance, and was constantly pushing his activities just to the edge of the law.

He didn't know who he was or where he was going in life, and as a result, he failed to concentrate on his studies and had to be held back a grade. This made him one of the oldest people in his class, and as it happened, he was the only one old enough to have a driver's license. He was the man with "wheels" and so he was very much in demand; boys liked to double-date and girls liked to embark on weekend adventures with him.

But as swashbuckling and fun-loving as this boy seemed to be on the outside, he was experiencing tremendous turmoil underneath. He vascillated between extremes. One week, he got involved in the prank of spraying shaving cream all over the cars in one neighborhood—and that brought him to the attention of the local police. The next week, he was moved at a local church service to make a decision to enter the ministry!

The forces of light and the forces of darkness were in intense conflict; this boy was an unintegrated, divided personality. That's not to say that he was "sick," or so emotionally disturbed that he needed to be institutionalized. He was just a rather extreme case of what happens when a youngster begins to move from childhood into adulthood and to consummate that ongoing process of independence that began in the late stages of infancy.

MANAGING THE CONFIDENCE CRISIS

Everybody, but *everybody*, goes through each of these confidence crises. Furthermore, the success with which we meet each of these challenges is a measure of the degree of our self-assurance.

But at the same time, there's a caveat: No parent should attempt to *force* a child through any of these crises! Rather, the child's own body and emotions, his changing perspective of the world as he grows, will bring on each phase.

In other words, as the crisis occurs, instead of trying to push a child into or through any one of these situations, the parent should remain relatively (and sometimes uncomfortably) in the background. Your role, as your child's main caretaker, should be mainly to assist and encourage him to fight his own battles.

How, specifically, can you help your youngster through these phases?

We'll be devoting considerable space to discussing some possible answers to this question. But even though each phase has its own peculiar problems and solutions, there are a few broad, general themes that are present in each.

Whether your child is five or fifteen, he or she may be one of the following:

- plagued by *fears*
- challenged by a need to have the courage of his convictions and
- confronted by the importance of distinguishing between absolutes and discretionary matters

Let's take a look at each of these broad themes and explore some ways that you can deal with them no matter what confidence crisis your child may be confronting.

Theme One: Fears

You want to crush your child's self-confidence?

One of the best tactics is a cavalier dismissal of his or her fears as "childish" or "silly." Any fear that a child harbors is too real to be discarded out-of-hand. There are countless fears and anxieties that plague children—so many, in fact, that psychologists have trouble keeping track of them.

Dr. Ruth Formanek, professor of education at Hofstra University and chief psychologist at the Jewish Community Services in Rico Park in Queens, New York, ran a computer check of professional papers on childish anxieties. Over a recent period of only three years, she came up with 2,000 titles!

As part of her research, she unearthed a study of the fears of 400 children that was done almost a half century ago at Teachers College, Columbia University.

"The ones that came up most frequently were animals, dark rooms, high places, strange persons, loud sounds, insecure footing and being left alone," she reported.

Dr. Formanek's research and that of other experts suggest strongly that many fears are universal among children. So they should be treated seriously and respectfully by parents, lest they be aggravated and begin to gnaw too voraciously at a child's self-confidence.

Sadly, in today's society children have come under attack by a whole fusillade of new fears.

"Somehow," says Dr. Formanek, "children seem to be more afraid now than they were in the past of parents getting divorced, of parents dying in an accident or because of a harmful practice, such as smoking or drug abuse. They are afraid of air pollution, of nuclear weapons."

One four-year-old demanded that his father, not his mother, accompany him to nursery school daily. The reason? Not so much affection, as fear. Many of his classmates in school, he explained, "have no daddy living at home and I'm scared that will happen to me."

Other studies have shown that children, especially those in urban areas, are afraid of being mugged by other children. They live in daily anxiety of physical attack: Many girls in these areas develop the fear of being raped even before they reach puberty.

How can you deal effectively and realistically with such fears? I'd recommend two basic steps:

1. Encourage your child to express his anxieties. Getting his feelings on the table will always go a long way towards eliminating the root of the fear. And sometimes the best way to do this is to share with the child something *you* have found troublesome.

    A father may sense that his son is being bothered by some fear. Just to get the conversation rolling, he might say: "You know, I used to be afraid of a lot of things when I was a little guy. The dark was something I really didn't like at all. But probably the worst thing for me was snakes. I was *really* afraid of snakes! How about you? Does anything make you a little afraid?"

    Such an open-ended, nonthreatening approach may open the

door to further communication between you and your child about deep-rooted fears.

An exhortation to "be a man, my son!" just won't do it! That approach certainly won't exorcise any fears, and it may very well shut off the possibility of any further disclosures from your child.

2.   After your child has begun to express herself, be sure that you deal with what you learn respectfully and sympathetically. Among other things, this means not undermining what you have accomplished by exposing her to the taunts or teasing of family or friends. You must learn that children also need confidentiality.

3.   Above all, parents should be reassuring about the stability of the family. Many experts believe that the Big Fear underlying all others is what's called "separation anxiety." This is a deep-rooted anxiety that one or both of the parents is somehow going to leave or disappear. After all, for most children the most secure place in all the world, for all its deficiencies and imperfections, is home. And the cornerstones of home are Mom and Dad.

Theme Two: The Courage of One's Convictions

An important aspect of anyone's self-confidence is the ability to have the courage of his convictions. Any time you're able to state *your* honest opinion, rather than to mimic or provoke the reaction of somebody else in the room, you display self-confidence.

"Here's a part of me that is *different*," you're saying. "This is *my* experience, *my* feeling—and I don't feel threatened if you don't agree with me."

Such an assertion doesn't come easily to any small child. For example, if you ask a toddler what his favorite thing is, he'll probably say, "I like it all, I like everything." He won't make any decisions that will show that he puts one issue or item above another.

Around the age of three or so, I noticed that my little daughter Bonnie would begin to blurt out spontaneously, "I love this!" or, "I like that!"

But she was still quite dependent on me. If I would say first, "I like *that*," she would mimic me. She'd say, "Oh, I like that, too! I love that!"

At this stage, a child is on the threshold of developing some independent opinions—an important feature of self-confidence. But she hasn't quite made it yet. She still won't say, "Oh, I really like that," or, "Well, I don't like that at all" if the parent doesn't agree.

Of course, things get very subtle at this stage of a child's development. The child is strongly influenced by a parent's opinions and is often reluctant to express *positive* likes or to present a hierarchy of favorite things to do or be. At the same time, a strong, creeping negativism begins to enter in during the toddler stage.

Take my daughter, for example. When she was two or three, I could ask her, "Bonnie, you like this cereal, don't you?"

Once I'd insert a negative possibility, I'd get it thrown right back in my face. "*No*, I *don't!*" she'd retort. But still, she might not be quite as certain as she sounded.

For example, she might have flatly refused to eat something she said she didn't like. But then I would take away her plate and start to eat the food myself.

"Oh, this is delicious!" I'd exclaim. "I *love* it."

Now, Bonnie would have some misgivings. She'd think maybe she'd missed something. And immediately she'd begin to plead, "Me some, Mommy, me some!"

Then, she would get the food into her mouth again and realize she was right the first time. So she'd spit it out.

The point here is that at this age she found it almost impossible to fly in the face of any strong conviction that I might express. She hadn't yet reached the courage of her own convictions, the courage to tell me, "You like it, Mom? Then *you* eat it!"

At the same time, when she began to balk at my suggestions, I knew I should welcome the negativism, despite any temporary exasperation I might feel. It was a sign that she was reaching toward greater self-confidence.

The same thing is true of any early negative phase that a child goes through. Every parent has experienced numerous situations, when a child is in the two- to four-year-old range, in which almost any parental suggestion will be met with a loud "no!" In fact, with many children, parents get used to expecting the child to give them a hard time about wearing certain clothes, going to certain events, or behaving in some particular way.

Obviously, the child has to learn to obey and follow. But these expressions of an independent will are important milestones in the child's ability to form an opinion about something and then have the guts and determination to stick with it.

Another early indication that your child is struggling to stand on her own two feet will be her increasing use of the personal pronoun. There's a world of difference between saying, "*I* like that," and saying, "That is good."

To make a universal statement like "That is good" implies that every normal, right-thinking person will feel the same way. A child who takes this approach is in effect going along with the crowd.

When your youngster says, "I like that," there's another implication: He's suggesting that although perhaps not everyone will feel the way he does, he still has an opinion. He's going to stick to his guns.

When Bonnie turned four, she got more opinionated. For example, if she had to make a decision, she would often say to me "What would *you* choose?" But she had developed the strength and self-knowledge either to take my choice *or* an alternative.

Expressions of independent opinion and judgment like this are *major* steps towards independence and self-confidence. So they should be respected, especially when a child first begins to talk this way. If you respond with some strong negative comment, an absolute that allows for no disagreement, or worse, with ridicule, that will make your youngster worry about putting himself on the line the next time around. And his self-confidence will suffer accordingly.

Theme Three: The Acceptance of Absolutes

I don't want to get bogged down here in metaphysics, but I do think it's important to emphasize to your child that there are certain absolutes in life. Your parental love for him is an absolute in the sense that he should regard it as something immovable and universal. It's something that will always be there, no matter what he does, what you do, or what other forces or people may enter your lives. That parental love isn't relative or discretionary. It's a fundamental fact of the cosmos.

I also believe that it's important to introduce other absolutes into your child's life in order to set him on a firm and secure path toward achievement, happiness and success. For example, there's a place for injunctions against lying, cheating and stealing—in *all* circumstances. Also, if you're religiously oriented, the assertion "God loves you" unconditionally, in all circumstances, is a tremendous confidence-builder.

Other absolutes may assume the form of practical rules of conduct and safety: I've always been big on such commandments as, "children should never cross the street alone" or, "children should never talk to strangers."

A child fortified by absolutes such as these will enjoy a firm bedrock upon which to build feelings of self-worth and self-confidence. Such a foundation can't be easily shaken, no matter what the challenges may be from the outside. Any youngster who has been firmly instructed—and has learned to trust—in the right set of absolutes will tend to be much more decisive. He'll be less easily confused when presented with difficult challenges in life.

Top executives in many of the nation's major corporations tend to follow the same approach, by the way. But a major difference is that instead of calling these "absolutes," they may call them "policies."

I know one chief executive officer who, besieged by invitations to make speeches to charitable organizations, told his secretary, "I'll only give 10 of these speeches a year. Four will be to these universities . . . " and he named them. "Four will be to religious groups, and the other two will have to be for major public charities."

By making this sort of decision ahead of time, this executive streamlined his decision making and eliminated a great deal of confusion from his life. Similarly, by helping your child to settle on certain actions that are right and certain ones that are wrong, you'll rescue him from a great deal of muddling around. Moreover, you'll do wonders for his self-confidence when he finds himself alone, having to stand up for certain values and practices in the face of challenges by his peers.

But again, here's a caveat: A child who believes only in absolutes that are established by someone else and lacks a sense of his own individuality certainly won't be truly self-confident. So there's a fine line on the one hand between having enough absolutes to encourage self-confidence and decisive action, and on the other, having so many absolutes that they strangle initiative and independent thinking. The challenge of parenting is to allow for growth and change without compromising the groundwork.

Still, I would err on the side of having too many rather than too few absolutes. One of the most deplorable aspects of child rearing these days is the reluctance or even fear on the part of so many parents to say, "This is right, and this is wrong!"

So many adults are unsure of their own beliefs that they are reluctant to try to tell their kids what they should or shouldn't do. They feel hypocritical in emphasizing any sort of absolute moral or ethical system, so they remain mute. The result is a surrender to permissiveness that has bred much of the disruptive despair of today's young people.

Remember: Every child goes through a phase, whether he openly expresses it or not, when he perceives Mom or Dad as having a sure, confident grasp on how the world works. Kids *expect* and need to get some moral instruction from their parents. If they don't get it, they're likely to feel that they're constantly at sea, floundering about in the threatening world.

Children without absolutes in their lives—or with values that are half-baked and half-formed—are psychological orphans. They can't possibly become confident about themselves because they lack firm basic assumptions about what is valuable and meaningful in the outside world. Parental desertion of this primary duty of passing on absolutes is one of the great tragedies of our time—all the more so, when many parents mean well but are too weak or ill-advised to *act* well.

A corollary to this acceptance of absolutes by a child is the necessity of discipline.

Now I know that discipline—and especially the word "punishment"—is viewed with scepticism in many homes, and in many schools, as well. Mother is often too tired or preoccupied to impose discipline. Father resents being cast in the role of the "enforcer" when he returns from work in the evening, and so he avoids it as well. It becomes even easier to avoid disciplining a child if you, as the parent, are rather unsure yourself about what is right and what is wrong.

Yet children not only require discipline; no matter how much they may grumble or protest, they actually *crave* it. Consider, for example, a recent eye-opening poll taken by *Read Magazine*, a National School Publication published by Xerox Education Publishers.

This publication, which goes to a half million students in junior and senior high schools across the country, surveyed more than 12,000 students. The poll found that four out of five believed that school violence could be reduced through discipline. Moreover, 87 percent said they would welcome "a lot of " or "some" discipline.

"Principals and teachers let kids break rules," one student from Beaver, Pennsylvania complained. "They say, 'Well, just this once we'll let it go.' But every time they let a kid get away with something, they make the situation worse for themselves, for the troublemaker and for the kids who want to learn something."

It's also important to place the ultimate responsibility in the right place. Classroom chaos is merely the logical extension of a failure at home to set rules and absolutes, and to enforce them.

A boy from New Jersey put his finger on the real problem when he said: "I think parental negligence—and lack of parental discipline—is at the root of it."

Out of the mouths of babes?

You'll find these three themes—overcoming fears, the courage of convictions, and absolutes—running through every phase of your child's progress toward significant self-confidence. So it's important always to keep them in mind and gently encourage and nurture them when the opportunity arises.

As you begin to help your child in these areas, you'll probably also find that you have to develop and fine-tune many of these qualities and strengths in yourself. But that's part of the personal growth and fun that comes from being a serious parent.

Now, let's turn back to that first basic crisis of confidence—the basic trust crisis. What exactly does that early phase in your child's self-confidence involve, and what can you do to help your youngster through it? To answer these and related questions, it's necessary to begin at the very beginning—the birth of your youngster and the months immediately following.

PART TWO

The Five Self-Confidence Crises

3

Crisis One: Developing a Basic Trust

During the first year or two of life, your baby will be seeking a successful answer to a key question that will shape his self-confidence in all the years to come:

CAN I TRUST MY ENVIRONMENT?

At this early stage, your youngster can't quite comprehend that he's separate from his environment. Rather, he assumes that anything that happens to him somehow comes from *inside* himself. His outside environment is actually an extension of his inner being, and so it's extremely important that the environment be secure and understandable to the youngster. Otherwise, the consequences for his self-confidence may be devastating.

One key issue that's related to early self-confidence can be stated, with apologies to Hamlet, as follows: "To cry or not to cry, that is the question."

TO CRY OR NOT TO CRY?

Both personally and professionally I have found that *the* most nagging question of all for new parents—after that first anxious query, "Is my baby normal?"—is, "Should I let her cry?"

In my own case, when my daughter, Bonnie, was very young, many people strongly cautioned me against picking her up when she began to wail. If I give in, they warned darkly, she would be a "spoiled" baby who would quickly begin to use crying to manipulate me.

But my maternal instincts told me to pick her up and cuddle her, even if she *was* doing a super-subtle job of manipulation. And in retrospect, I know I was right. In fact, we mothers have been doing a lot of things right just by following those instinctive urges about child care, long before there were pediatricians or child psychologists to coach us.

But being a trained physician, I wasn't willing to go completely on what my instincts told me, no matter how strongly they urged me to scoop Bonnie up and hug her to my breast. So I went to the medical literature, and sure enough, I found *massive* studies to support what my own insides had told me was right. It seems Mother *does* know best. The literature is quite consistent in saying, in effect: "Pick up your infant and soothe her when she cries. That won't spoil her!"

For example, take the formidable *The Modification of Social Responsiveness in Institutional Babies*, a monograph by H.L. Rheingold for The Society for Research and Child Development published in 1965. This tome, which certainly wouldn't be accessible to most mothers, nevertheless supports the maternal impulse to respond to the crying child. Moreover, the monograph suggests that a proper response to a child's signal, such as crying, makes him more willing and less afraid to explore strange environments and new situations.

Also, I found that medical research tends to debunk the notion that a crying baby is seeking to manipulate his primary caretaker. Instead, his howls and screams are efforts to determine if that environment is responsive to his needs. And the main representative of that environment is Mom or her representative. When the youngster cries, he really *does* need to be picked up and reassured.

Of course, there comes a point with the bawling infant when you have tried everything. All the picking up, walking the floor and shushing just hasn't worked. You may have to let him cry it out or get outside help. But this hands-off approach must not become the pattern of responsiveness (or unresponsiveness) that you establish with the infant.

By and large, during the first six months of life, you should assume that your youngster's cry is a cry for help, and *not* just a mere clamoring for attention. The help she needs could be physical, such as dry diapers or food. Just as important, however, that wailing may be for emotional support and reassurance. A warm and loving touch from the parent may be just the thing to assure a youngster all is really right with the world.

Most modern physicians who have been schooled in how to handle a crying child will advise parents in these terms:

1. Don't ignore the cry! Check the child out.
2. Assume first that something is wrong. Determine whether he seems to be hungry, is wet, is developing diaper rash or is just lying in an uncomfortable position. To find the source of the problem, you'll obviously have to check the condition of your child closely and monitor feeding times, just to see if the time has arrived for a snack or meal. Imagine if you had to tell someone else every time you needed to roll over in bed! Or perhaps the youngster's needs are emotional: In that case, simply pick him up, hug him and walk around a little bit. That may help to soothe and calm him.
3. *Don't* just offhandedly decide that your youngster is behaving like a "spoiled brat." Many child-rearing experts feel that you can't spoil a child who is eight months old or younger, and I'm inclined to agree. Providing a youngster with reassuring contact isn't going to spoil him. It's going to make him feel secure and good about himself—and you.

What any pediatrician with these attitudes is recommending is that your baby's inner core of self-confidence should be bolstered by encouraging confidence in his environment. Moreover, such confidence can be established only through a *consistent* relationship with that environment. As your child sends out his "test-signals" with a cry or a wail the repetition of your response to him will show him that the world is a relatively predictable and positive place. All self-confidence begins with positive expectations about what you as individuals can do with and through your surroundings.

So, in many ways, the journey to self-confidence begins with an infant's cry for help. A baby will begin to believe in himself when he sees that his important signals like crying, smiling or cooing result in positive and pleasant responses. But there are many issues besides crying that highlight the basic trust crisis. A key one is the role of nurturing adults in the baby's life.

What Kind of Caretaker?

As your child grapples with that fundamental question, "Can I trust my own environment?" he unconsciously poses some very tough questions for his caretakers!

*   Is it enough for a youngster to be brought up in a bright, pleasant environment among people who like children—even if they aren't parents?
*   Should a baby be nurtured by one person rather than many in a group setting, no matter how well meaning the members of that group?
*   Is there some sort of mystical "bonding" that takes place between parent and child in these early months?

These are certainly tough questions, and I don't want to suggest that I've got any simple, easy answers. But I do want to emphasize one point: I believe strongly that there's something special about the relationship between a child and its mother.

When I first began to work in a hospital, I assumed that it didn't really make much difference *who* responded to a child's cry, just so long as *someone* did. Now, I know better.

There's no doubt in my mind that an infant recognizes almost at birth some one, special individual who is most sensitive to his or her needs. And in most cases, as we've already seen, that special person tends to be the mother. Even the youngest premature infants, with whom I've worked a great deal in hospitals, respond more quickly and enthusiastically to their mothers than even to the most sensitive nurse.

T. Berry Brazelton and other medical researchers have shown that even "preemies" born a month too early can distinguish between the male and female voice. If a man and woman both speak at the same time, the infant will consistently turn to the woman, not the man.

Other studies have refined the degree of this sensitivity even more. Suppose that two women, one who is the mother and one who is not, talk to an infant. Even if the infant is too young to control his head and turn toward the mother, his eyes will seek her out.

Doctors and nurses in the nation's most up-to-date infant-care facilities recognize the importance of the primary caretaker, and especially of the mother, in the life of these newborns. As a result, hospital staffs try to maximize the time that parents, and especially mothers, are able to spend with their babies.

A great deal has been written in recent years about the concept of "bonding." This concept, known as the Klaus-Kennell theory after the doctors who formulated it, can best be stated in these physicians' own words:

"There is a sensitive period in the first minutes and hours of life during which it is necessary that the mother and father have close contact with their neonate for later development to be optimal."

In their later writings, in response to criticisms of the bonding concept, Klaus and Kennell have changed their positions somewhat. In particular, they emphasize that if parents and children miss the early bonding experience right after birth, they can make up for it later in their relationship. As the doctors put it: "The human is highly adaptable and there are many fail-safe routes to attachment."

But whether you call it bonding or something else, there seems to be no doubt that a mother's presence from the earliest possible point of existence is tremendously reassuring to the youngster.

Take a simple situation that almost everyone is familiar with. If an infant is put into a strange room, he's much more likely to crawl about to explore it if he knows his mother is nearby. For example, if the mother is in a room with the child, the youngster is much more likely to head for an adjoining room and look it over, especially if he can keep looking over his shoulder to see that his mother is still in view.

Intermittently, as this exploration is taking place, the youngster will probably head back to his mother for some physical contact. Or he may just sit up and cry until she comes over and reassuringly pats him. Her mere presence will contribute to his sense of self-confidence in relaunching his "expedition" into unfamiliar territory.

I don't want to be simplistic about this and suggest that I believe that a child should never be alone, never away from her mother. Each child will react differently, just as each one will go through various steps of development at a special, individual speed.

Also, the main figure or caretaker, the "significant other," in a youngster's life, doesn't *have* to be the mother. It could be the father, the grandparents or even a baby-sitter. After all, there are many societies in the world where a "nanny" has provided the primary nurturing role during the early years. These include the upper class in Great Britain, the wealthy in certain parts of the United States and the middle class and upper-middle class in the southern United States only a few decades ago.

Because there are many precedents of someone other than the mother taking care of a child during its very early years, some parents may ask, quite logically: Does it really matter whether a child has one or more caretakers in the early years, just so long as they're all warm and loving? In fact, might it not instill an *extra* sense of self-confidence in a youngster if he has a lot of extra loving individuals caring for him?

At a later stage of a child's development, say from about age three on, I would answer yes to these questions. But in early infancy, the differences among various individuals, even if they are very loving and supportive, could be disconcerting to a baby. He responds to many things about an individual, including the body smell, the shape of the face and how the face moves. Too much variety may be confusing and unsettling. And the last thing you want to do is to threaten a youngster's emerging self-confidence with confusing and unsettling conditions.

Of course, after the groundwork is laid with a one-on-one relationship, other attachments can and should follow. Also, recent research indicates that if an infant's attachment to the main figure or caretaker in his life is especially strong, he'll be more likely to develop secondary attachments to other people.

Now, let me say something that is going to be even more unpopular: During the first year or so of life, I strongly object to putting an infant in a setting where he's subjected to multiple caregivers for most of his waking hours. I'm talking here about day-care centers and nursery schools, which are totally inadequate substitutes for a mother's love and attention at that very young age.

I realize that in some cases economic necessity allows no other choice. But if there's any other way to avoid the multiple caregiver solution, I would highly recommend that you follow it.

So what's a career-oriented mother to do?

The optimum solution is for the mother to interrupt her career and remain home with the child. But before some of you erupt with irritation and even rage at such an old-fashioned suggestion, let me explain. I know that in many cases this solution will prove impossible or unfeasible. So if you feel you can't stay at home with your youngster, you must try to seek out an environment that is as close as possible to what your child could enjoy in a traditional home setting with a mother present.

If you have the cash (but no family volunteers), there seem to be two viable possibilities:

- A nanny or governess comes into your home, lives with your children and focuses her attention upon them.
- Your child is entrusted to a baby-sitter in the sitter's home, where only a *very* small number of children are being cared for. If the number of children in such a situation exceeds two or three, your youngster is really in a day-care setting.

But these two solutions are not by any means ideal.

Take the first: the nanny or governess approach. Too often, as one wag has put it, "In the age of the two-income family, parent and nursemaid are two ships that pass in the foyer."

The problem, in other words, is that after a fairly lengthy hiring interview, there may be precious little communication between the mother and the nanny. This lack of in-depth discussion takes on increasing significance as the charge grows and his emotional and physical needs begin to change radically.

One former nursery schoolteacher, Susan Kurnit, says that this mother-nanny relationship may become "almost like a marriage in which the partners fail to communicate along the way. If they don't talk continually about their needs and their expectations and what's going on in the development of the child, anger builds up on both sides and the relationship falls apart."

The nanny may become resentful. Perhaps she feels she's been taken for granted or is being forced to assume domestic chores like cleaning and laundry, which weren't part of the original deal. On the other hand, if she becomes *too* successful with the child, the *mother* may become resentful.

As Mrs. Kurnit puts it: "When the person is too good, too wonderful, in the back of your head you're jealous. Some of this has to do with the guilt and ambivalence mothers feel about leaving their children to go to work."

Another ongoing problem with nursemaids is that they tend to change their jobs fairly regularly, often at intervals of about eighteen months to two years. Such a succession of nannies may bewilder a small child and in turn threaten his self-confidence. He wonders and worries what he's doing wrong to cause that nanny who seemed to love him so much to leave.

Because of the difficulties that surround the nanny solution, I personally prefer placing the child with a responsible baby-sitter in the sitter's own home.

In part, as I've indicated previously, my choice of this option is firmly rooted in my own experience: I worked full time, five days a week, eight to six o'clock, as a practicing neonatologist and pediatrician during the first year and a half of life of my elder child, my daughter Bonnie. During that time, I put Bonnie with another mother who had a three-and-a-half-year-old child of her own. For all practical purposes, this woman was the main mothering figure for Bonnie during that first year.

Quite frankly, at the time I didn't realize the full impact of what I was doing. If someone had told me, "You know, Jean, you're no longer the mother of that child—the sitter is," I would have been shocked.

But I know now that I was not the primary caretaker during that period of time. I was not the one who was having the greatest impact on Bonnie's day-to-day development. In short, I was not the one who was having the greatest input into the development of her self-confidence.

This factor has become more and more apparent to me as Bonnie has grown older and her little brother, Keith, has come into the world. I've seen during the first year of Keith's life how many opportunities there are for the mother or caregiver to provide a secure environment for the development of self-confidence. In retrospect, I realize how much I really "lucked out" in the kind of arrangement that I settled upon during Bonnie's first year.

Her surrogate mother during that year turned out to be a very loving lady, who had only two children to care for. There was no group of kids to divert her attention and love away from both her child and my own.

The bottom line for me is that the groundwork for self-confidence must be laid—and must be laid *securely*—at the very earliest stages of life. Moreover, you will find it very difficult to make up later for failure to give your child a secure start in life.

Admittedly, this position of mine is rather controversial. Some authorities have proclaimed that if you must be away from your baby at some point, then it's best to be away earlier rather than later, when the child is more aware of what's going on around him. One flaw in this early absence theory has been pointed up by new findings that a child begins to learn during very early infancy. And as the early learning is taking place, the child's human relationships are extremely important.

In his book *Clinical Aspects of Child Development*, Melvin Lewis notes that the attachments to other children and significant adults like nursery schoolteachers and family friends doesn't really begin to get strong in a child's life until about the third year. Most important, it's only at this relatively late age that the secondary attachments become strong enough to compensate for a mother's absence.

One of the reasons that the mother is so important in these early years is that in many cases, she's the only one who really cares enough to give the child the kind of attention he deserves and craves. It's easier for a tired or cranky caregiver to ignore a child who's a little hungry, tired, uncomfortable, irritable—or even sick or in pain. After all, if the only ones present are the adult nursemaid and a child who's not even old enough to talk, who will be able to tell the tale to the parents if there's the little slippage in the quality of care?

It may seem callous and untrusting to make an observation like this. But I think it's important to be realistic. Most likely, nobody is going to go that extra mile with your youngster the way you yourself would.

Yet for your child to have the most complete, positive and enriching experience in those early years, all her basic physical and emotional needs have to be met. If the basic physical and emotional conditions haven't been provided, then a youngster is not going to be in a position to explore, enjoy and wonder at his environment.

Also, young infants need a great deal of personal attention, physical contact and positive stimulation to feel confident about their surroundings. You have to "pick 'em up . . . coo to 'em . . . and talk regularly to 'em," if you hope to get the youngest children excited about their environment.

And believe me, these extra efforts to give your youngsters plenty of attention won't be wasted. You may not be able to teach them the difference between colors when they're only a few months old, but by offering them bright cards and toys and a variety of textures for them to test against their own touch, you'll *definitely* be providing them with a richer, more interesting environment. Most of all, you'll be establishing a stable context that will help foster self-confidence.

Although the role of the adult human caretaker is crucial to the emerging self-confidence of a very young child, certain inanimate objects may also assume a position of unusual importance in the child's feelings of assurance and self-esteem. One of these is the so-called "security blanket."

THE SECURITY BLANKET SIGNAL

If we're honest, most of us will admit to leaning on some crutch to get us through the rough periods in life. Sometimes, it's a tangible talisman or good luck charm that we may carry with us to bolster our self-confidence. The golfer with the lucky shirt or the businessman with the lucky tie are classic examples.

Children facing the Basic Trust Crisis have many of the same tendencies, but their "good luck charm" is often called a "security blanket." Sometimes, the blanket is actually a blanket—a piece of cloth, wool or felt that a child carries around just to be reassured that all is right with the world. With other children, the security object may be a pacifier, toy or some other item. In my family, we had a teddy bear with one arm and no eyes. Despite its obvious physical deficiencies, we all felt reassured when that teddy was somewhere near us.

There's nothing wrong with this kind of ego booster, just so long as when push comes to shove, the youngster can do without it. Also, it's important for the child to outgrow the security blanket, usually before the preschool years are over.

But sometimes, an emotionally dangerous kind of attachment develops: A child may really believe he needs his relationship with this object in order to continue to exist. In other words, the object takes on such significance that the child really can't function without it.

This phenomenon occurs when an adult close to the child—say, the mother—lets him down in some way. The security blanket may also become extremely important in tragedies, as when a member of a child's family has been killed in an accident.

Youngsters may also develop the need for a security blanket when the sibling salvos begin to intensify. In other words, a youngster may feel severely threatened by the presence of a younger or older brother or sister. If the parents have failed to fill in the void of security that this child feels, a security device of some type may enter to occupy the vacuum.

I'm reminded of one little two-year-old boy who was constantly being ordered about and bullied by his four-year-old brother. The older child was quite pushy and physical, and that caused the younger to feel that he was constantly in danger of having his little world upset. Because the parents didn't step in often enough to defend him, the younger boy began to seek security and reassurance in a little stuffed dog.

This state of affairs went on for more than a year, until the parents finally realized that their younger son was relying on this security device much more than other children they knew. Without even understanding all the dynamics between the younger and the older boy, they simply began to focus more of their attention on the younger one—with the result that the "security dog" became less and less important to him.

I know another child who lost almost all his possessions in a fire in his home—with the exception of one or two toys. Now he *absolutely* will not part with those toys. Any effort to take them away causes such a major reaction that he seems to fear that his own existence is actually being threatened.

Normally, the need for the security blanket will vanish naturally—or the shabby old thing will get lost; the child will go through a couple of rough days and then get on with the rest of his life. But whatever you do, don't assume that there's a deadline by which a blanket, pacifier or other security device has to go. Each child marches to a different drummer, as far as his developing self-confidence is concerned. You have to learn to listen to that drummer and respond accordingly.

Furthermore, be sure that you don't make a special effort to get rid of the security blanket just after a new baby has arrived in the home. It's just plain cruel to pull out this important prop, which helps support the older child at the very time when he is experiencing his initial sibling challenge.

Also, it's important to be alert to other items or practices that may serve the same function as the security blanket. We've already mentioned toy animals and pacifiers. In addition, there may be rituals or litanies, especially at bedtime, which can serve the same function.

I know one little boy who repeats a fixed litany every night just before he goes to sleep. It's extremely important to him that he get all the way through it and that his mother respond appropriately. He'll say, "There aren't going to be any fireworks tonight, Mommy?"

She has to respond, "No."

"The stars and moon will be out, even if they're behind the clouds?"

Answer, "Yes."

In the past, these points have assumed particular importance to him during discussions with his parents, and he wants to be reassured that the answers are still the same. Then, he has to get his juice at the right moment, say his prayers and have the light turned out precisely on cue. If the routine is disturbed in any way, *he* gets disturbed, and he has trouble going to sleep.

In an adult, such behavior might be regarded as highly neurotic or compulsive. But in a young child, especially a three- or four-year-old, this sort of litany or ritual is quite common. Behind it all is the need for assurance that Mommy—or Daddy—is always there, ready to respond in a predictable, predetermined way. The ritual makes the child feel more secure, and it undoubtedly helps to lay the groundwork for greater self-confidence in the future.

If the need for the security item persists stubbornly through the later preschool years, even in the face of possible derision by other children, then I still wouldn't take it away. Rather, I'd ask, "How can I make my child feel more secure? What can I do to strengthen his self-confidence?"

He's obviously signaling that he needs a boost to his inner self. Often, you give that "confidence injection" to him and help make up for the blanket simply by giving him more of yourself, more of your time, energy and attention.

THE GREAT BREAST-FEEDING BATTLE

Another big issue that has significant implications for the evolving self-confidence of a very young child focuses on breast-feeding. There have been many battles over the years about breast-feeding.

But one incontrovertible fact is that this practice has become increasingly popular in recent years.

In the early 1970s, fewer than 25 percent of new mothers were nursing. Less than a decade later, according to the National Center For Health Statistics, more than half were doing so. And more mothers were nursing for a year or more than in the past.

But as I say, there have been many questions concerning the practice of breast-feeding. These range from whether or not you should do it to how long you should do it; to the circumstances under which you should do it—e.g., should you feed with breast milk alone or a combination of the milk and solid foods?

Another problem that may arise for mothers who breast-feed is what to do if they have a second child before the first has been weaned. In other words, suppose that you're still nursing your two-year-old when your new baby comes along. Should you try to nurse both of them at the same time? Or should you wean the first and move on to the second? Then again, might it be advisable just to bottle-feed the second and continue breast-feeding the first until he gets tired of the breast?

There are no clear-cut answers to these questions. But let me offer a simple game plan for those mothers who are breast-feeding in a family of two or more young children.

First of all, I'd suggest that you consider weaning your child at least by the time he's between ages one and one and a half. This way, you'll be better prepared if a second child comes along unexpectedly. You can usually complete the weaning process for the older youngster fairly efficiently and still have a few months to go before the next birth. The newborn can then begin breast-feeding without the first feeling that he is being shoved aside.

In any case, I think it might be disasterous to wait until the last moment to wean your first child and then immediately put the second on the breast in his place. If your first is in the "terrible twos" phase, as he most likely will be, you'll probably be confronted with a series of explosions and perhaps some difficult emotional problems as a result of pushing him aside.

A number of nutrition experts agreee with Dr. Myron Winick, the head of the Institute of Human Nutrition at Columbia-Presbyterian Medical Center, who says, "There is no reason from a nutritional standpoint why one cannot continue to breast-feed children for a relatively long time."

On the other hand, a child gains some of the major nutritional benefits of breast-feeding relatively early in life. For the great majority of children, the unique benefits of breast milk—i.e., protection against allergies and certain infections—are conferred mainly during the first six months to a year, when the child is receiving most of his nutrition as breast milk.

There are also practical, non-nutritional considerations: The mother with two children may find it impossible to meet the simultaneous demands of physical hunger of an infant and emotional hunger of the toddler. Bottle or cup feeding may allow another special person—e.g., a father or grandparent—to provide cuddling and extra attention in a lap other than Mommy's.

Finally, there are important psychological issues. For example, Dr. Judd Marmor, past president of the American Psychiatric Association, notes, "I look askance at nursing children until they are two or three because it perpetuates the infantilizing of the child. Mothers who do this may have difficulty letting the child go."

But remember: Very little is known about the impact of lengthy breast-feeding on a child—especially about the impact on his self-confidence. If you decide to breast-feed for a long time and you have only one child, I would simply recommend that you monitor the development of that youngster in other areas of his life. If he seems to be getting along well, there's probably no reason not to continue the practice up to about age two or three, so long as both of you like it.

On the other hand, if a second child should be born during this period, I would strongly recommend that you allow at least six months between the time the first child is completely weaned and the second child starts on your breast. Otherwise, you may unwittingly contribute to the intensity of sibling conflicts in your family.

These, then, are some of the major issues that every parent will confront during the first phase of a child's emerging self-confidence, the Basic Trust Crisis. Clearly, these are not theoretical concepts or situations. They all have practical implications that put every parent on the line and call for important, life-shaping decisions.

In short, you should plan early-on what you intend to do about shaping your child's environment. That means beginning to take action right from day one. Don't fall into the trap of taking your child's life for granted. Also, don't assume that because he's so young, his environment won't have that much of an impact on him. Believe me, the earlier you give him regular, stimulating and loving attention, the earlier you'll see the effect on his development of self-confidence.

4

Crisis Two:
The Traumatic
Transition
to Toddlerhood

When your child passes his first birthday, he's well on his way to becoming a toddler. That is, he's a little human being who is just learning how to walk, talk and, in general, make his first major moves toward independence.

This is an exciting, stimulating time for a youngster. But it also involves a traumatic transition when he finds that he's no longer quite the center of the universe that he thought he was. In fact, as he moves on toward ages two and three, he'll probably discover that cute infants who "goo" or are on the verge of walking are getting much of the attention that used to be directed toward him.

Also, your child's language skills will probably begin to accelerate at a rapid rate during this phase. As a consequence, he'll not only hear and learn positive, helpful things; he'll also get plenty of negative feedback about his actions and abilities. This period of transition, then, will involve all sorts of new challenges and developments, and may very well present a tremendous threat to your youngster's fledgling self-confidence.

For the parent, there are two major challenges during this movement through toddlerhood. The first focuses on how you deal with his negative, contrary attitudes toward you and others. The second phase centers on how you help your youngster use his growing language abilities to become more assured and secure.

THE TERRIBLE TWOS: CAN YOU TURN A NEGATIVE TODDLER INTO A POSITIVE THINKER?

Sometime in the period between eighteen months and two-and-a-half years, your child will embark upon that exasperating adventure that's rightly been called "the terrible twos."

This is a period of supreme parent-child friction—with periodic explosions, the likes of which you'll probably not experience again until your youngster becomes a teenager.

Interestingly, there are similarities between what's happening to your child as a toddler and what will happen later during his teen years. At both times, your youngster will struggle to assert his individuality and independence. And of course, there's nothing wrong with that—as long as these tendencies can be channeled in the right direction. The more you can direct these drives rather than fight them, the more you'll help your youngster develop his self-confidence.

For my daughter, a maddening wave of negativism came with dramatic suddenness at the age of one and a half. It appeared to spring up overnight. One morning, Bonnie seemed to wake up knowing for the first time how to say "no!"—with a vengeance—to almost everything, including things that she really wanted!

With other children, this development may appear earlier or it may pop up later; it may come more slowly and subtly. But the result will usually be the same: Your child will constantly test her environment, her parents and herself.

Why do youngsters go through the "terrible twos?"

In effect, your toddler is saying to you, "What are the rules? *You* tell *me*. And if you don't, I'll push you until you do!"

But this message is not always what comes across very clearly. In fact, you'll sometimes really begin to wonder whether or not there *is* any message, other than obnoxious contrariness. You may also wonder if the importance of obeying family rules will ever register in that rebellious little mind.

But trust me: Sometime later, at the age of three to four, your patience will bear fruit. You'll begin to hear your child parrot his version of the rules you've given him during the terrible twos. In his own way, he will have internalized these principles of living and will be in the process of using them as a tool in mastering his world.

To get your points about good conduct and proper values across during this phase, you have to push through that powerful, offensive word—no—that keeps hitting you between the eyes. Yet you have to do it in a way that will bolster your child's self-confidence, rather than weaken his struggle for self-assertion.

Now, permit me to make two rather cheerful generalizations, which you most likely won't believe unless you already have some experience with a two-year-old:

* The negative responses you get from your child are signaling a positive development. In the case of most two-year-olds, this may at first seem to be an absurd statement. But it isn't, as we'll see shortly.
* The "no-no-no" stage really isn't as difficult for parents as it's cracked up to be—especially when you compare it with the drinking, driving, drugs and sex that you'll encounter during the teen years. But again, I don't expect you to believe this completely until you go through it.

Just why does a child become so ornery at the age of about eighteen months to two years?

During infancy, before he became independently mobile and learned to walk, your youngster had perceived himself as the *center* of the world. He did not understand or care about other people's feelings. So far as he was concerned, the rest of the world existed because of him. *He* created it, and that was that!

This infantile ego trip is sometimes referred to as "the all-powerful or omnipotent stage" in a child's development. But that all ends when he starts learning how to walk. Gradually, he sees himself not as the sun of his little solar system, but rather as a satellite of somebody else—in most cases, his mother.

This primary caretaker looms all-powerful, the one who determines everything in the child's life. Your youngster now begins to find out that he is not the be-all and end-all of existence; rather, he's a separate little thing having to compete with other separate things.

Try to put yourself into his baby shoes at this point. Kind of terrifying, isn't it?

Suddenly, everything is not responsive to him. He also begins to sense that Mom and Dad may not always be there when he needs them. At the same time, the child begins to undergo a kind of push-pull phenomenon in his family. He finds himslef pulled into the family as an important, accepted member; yet he also begins to push away in many ways as he asserts his own identity.

Admittedly, medical and psychological specialists don't know how much of this phase involves conscious action on the part of the child. But there's no doubt that the child is becoming aware, often in a highly painful way, that a traumatic transition is taking place in his life. That feeling can have serious repercussions for his sense of security and his belief in his own personal powers.

During this period in your child's life, it's important to learn to interpret the signals he's conveying to you about his own sense of confidence or lack thereof. Sometimes, the process of interpreting the meaning of your child's words and actions can be quite subtle and difficult.

For example, when he says, "I don't want this," or "I don't want to do that," it doesn't mean he's shying away from the outside world. Instead, he may be displaying a great deal of security about his environment. His "I-don't-wants" may be translated into, "I know you love me. And I know that, on faith, I can test your limits and see what kind of a behavior is acceptable."

At this point, the parents' own sense of self-confidence becomes quite important. It will be up to you to lay down some rules so that your child understands just how far he can go.

A child needs—indeed *craves*—some consistent basis for action when his whole view of himself is changing. But during a major transition phase such as the one to toddlerhood, feelings of inadequacy, confusion or inconsistency may become overwhelming—unless the parent is able to lay down the ground rules by which the game of the young child's life is to be played.

Part of these ground rules will involve the imposition of sanctions when the rules are disobeyed. Discipline becomes particularly important as a child moves through toddlerhood because this is the stage of life when he's beginning to build his ability to socialize and deal effectively with other people. If you don't teach him proper behavior with others, and enforce the basic principles that you establish, then your youngster will ultimately be the one who suffers.

For example, I found I couldn't expect my two-year-old son Keith to use his spoon and fork like an adult, or even like a more fastidious toddler. Nor could I expect him to cut his meat or otherwise observe all points of acceptable etiquette. But I *could*, and *did*, demand that he not throw his food around when he sat at the table.

Another rule that I began to drill into my children, even at this young age, was that they should *never* try to cross the street in front of our house alone. In fact, they were prohibited from even setting foot on the street. If they disobeyed, they had to be punished in some way—such as by losing their TV privileges for a time.

Every parent has bottom-line rules of this type that they formulate both for the child's social development and also for his safety. Enforcing these rules with firm discipline when they're broken doesn't undercut the child's self-confidence. Rather, these imperatives help lay the groundwork for a firm and mature sense of identity as the children get older.

In dealing with young children in my practice, as well as in rearing my own two youngsters, I've come up with a series of "tips" that have helped both me and others get through this traumatic transition of toddlerhood. Look them over and see if you don't find that many of them apply to your own situation.

Tip #1: Establish a Firm Family Policy on Limits and Discipline

At an early age, your child should get some clear ideas about how he's supposed to operate in your family. He has to understand what conduct is acceptable and what conduct is unacceptable. He must learn what actions involve acceptable risks and which ones are too dangerous.

An excessively permissive upbringing is especially sad because the child lacks guidance and instruction about common social and moral issues and attitudes. Children who are permitted to develop their own notions of right or wrong may become isolated and never really have a sense of being part of a family group. That sense of isolation or "being at sea" on the important issues of life will tend to make a child uncertain about his decision making—and less self-confident than he might otherwise be.

On the other hand, it's important to strike a balance between setting limits on behavior and being too rigid in trying to control everything the child does. Also, it's important to choose the right sanctions that will be appropriate for any given offense and will help the child grow into a secure, well-adjusted adult personality.

How can you establish firm family policies about behavior, communicate those policies effectively to the child and discipline her lovingly when she gets out of line?

1. Establish family policies on limits and disciplines.

   In this regard, it's helpful to sit down some evening and spend an hour or so thinking through those limits you want to set on your child's behavior. Has he been playing too often near or on a precarious bookcase in your living room? If there's no way you can make the bookcase safer, you may have to make that bookcase absolutely off limits to the youngster for his own health and safety.

   I know one family who had just this problem, and from the time their toddler first started to walk, the parents said authoritatively, "No!" when the youngster headed in the direction of the bookcase. Sometimes, of course, the child would test the parents' resolve and move over and put his hand on the bookcase. At those times, the mother or father would grab the child's hand fairly firmly, look directly into the youngster's eyes, tap the hand lightly but firmly and, once again, say "No!"

   This child soon learned that the bookcase was absolutely off limits to him, and soon he never bothered venturing in that direction. He wanted to please his parents, and they made it clear, without any equivocation, that he *wouldn't* be pleasing them if he touched that bookcase. Amazingly, this child is now seven years old, and *still* never goes near that bookcase! It's not that he's afraid of it or that he dislikes books; in fact, he's an avid, precocious reader. But the lesson that was taught him at an early age managed to keep him out of danger during those vulnerable years of toddlerhood.

2. When you discipline or correct a child, always focus on changing the child's inner motives and attitudes, rather than simply on his outward behavior.

Obviously, as a parent you're going to be quite interested in your child's outward behavior. But you'll never have a long-term, beneficial impact on that outward behavior unless you focus on what's going on inside your youngster.

Some interesting research along these lines has been conducted by Dr. Sanford M. Dornbusch, a researcher at California's Stanford University. In this survey of nearly 9,000 students, 3,500 parents and 500 teachers in San Francisco Bay area high schools, the researchers explored how parents' reactions could have an effect on the grades earned by their children. In general, the researchers found that when parents reacted negatively to bad report cards, their children tended to get relatively poor grades and also the grades tended to decline over time. In addition, when parents meted out punishment for poor grades, their children made lower grades.

Interestingly, even those children who received rewards for getting good grades got lower grades than their peers and also showed a decline in their school performance.

In contrast, what *does* work is the low-key, positive reponse, Dr. Dornbusch said. He noted that this approach involves offering praise for positive achievements by the child; encouraging the child to do better where he's weak; and offering parental assistance.

Dr. Dornbusch said that his findings reinforce research that has been done on nursery school students by a Stanford psychology professor, Dr. Mark Lepper. With these children, as with the high school students, it seems promising an external reward tends to make the child focus on the reward and not the learning. In contrast, the parents are much more effective in encouraging their children to raise their grades and school performance when they express concern for the child's welfare, offer to help and in general focus on the "intrinsic motive" involved in what the child is doing.

3. Settle on an intelligent, fair policy of punishment when you're in a calm mood and not in the heat of an argument with your youngster.

I would say that this point is applicable to any type of punishment, but especially to corporal punishment. Various studies have shown that more than 90 percent of all parents spank their children. But, unfortunately, many of them do this out of frustration or because they've run out of other ways to discipline the children.

In a study of parents of 186 children, ranging in age from five to eight years, in Portsmouth, New Hampshire, Barbara Carson of the University of New Hampshire's Family Research Laboratory discovered considerable uncertainty in the parents about their mode of discipline. She found that 83 percent of the parents spanked their children, but 40 percent felt that this physical punishment was seldom if ever effective. In fact, nearly 1/3 of the parents felt that they, the parents, were to blame for the spanking!

Carson concluded that in many cases, the resort to spanking reflected a loss of control on the part of the parents.*

The approach to limits, discipline and punishment that you begin early in your child's life will likely set the standard for your relationship in later years. It's extremely important for your youngster's emotional development that he or she understand as precisely as possible what the limits are and what the sanctions are likely to be if those limits are crossed. If you tend to punish inconsistently or primarily when you're angry, your youngster will find herself operating in a world with uncertain moral and behavioral guidelines. Such uncertainty can only bode ill for the development of a solid sense of self-confidence.

Tip #2: Choose Your Child's Friends

Sound rather dictatorial and high-handed? Perhaps so, if you're dealing with an older youngster. But with a toddler, you have to take a firm hand in managing the kinds of peers with whom he associates. Otherwise, you're likely to find that your child is being subjected to influences you don't agree with, influences that may serve to undercut his growing self-confidence.

One sensitive young boy was quite gregarious and operated quite well with the large majority of youngsters his own age. But occasionally he would encounter an overbearing playmate who seemed to stifle his creativity and independent judgment.

This boy would become cowed by the presence of one other child in particular. Finally, his mother and father decided that the associa-

* See *Psychology Today*, January 1985, p. 16

tion was doing far more harm than good. As a result, they started coming up with excuses and alternative activities to put the boy in situations where he wouldn't encounter his rather obnoxious, domineering peer.

I am quite sympathetic and supportive of the action these parents took. In fact, you're always justified in limiting your child's association with other youngsters who are a bad influence.

But let me suggest a few guidelines to keep in mind when you find yourself in this type of situation.

- I'm talking here about *limiting*, not entirely eliminating, contact with the other child. Some experience with adverse situations may be useful in helping your child learn to cope with difficulties.
- The limiting of contact should be done with kindness and sensitivity toward the other child. If your child picks up your feelings, he may broadcast them in a hurtful way toward the other youngster.
- Be honest with yourself and with your child's own inclinations. Your youngster may not always be the leader. He may select companions who are not your first choice, but who may be children with whom he feels comfortable.
- Sometimes, you can alter a negative situation by promoting activities which downplay offensive traits in a particular child. For example, you might emphasize games like ''Freeze Tag'' or ''Giant Steps'' instead of games that require skill and highlight developmental differences between children.
- Adults, rather than children, may be the source of the problem. For example, an adult relative may make negative comparisons between two children, and this may lead to problems in the relationship. In such a case, it's helpful for one of the other adults to speak privately with that person and try to correct her attitude and behavior. If this approach doesn't work, then you may have to resort to limiting contact between the children, at least in the presence of that adult.

Obviously, you can't completely control your youngster's relationships and interactions with other children, even at this very young age. But most parents do have considerably more power in this regard than they typically exercise.

Unfortunately, the children who are designated as "undesirable"—and who are avoided by parents who are sensitive to the problem of bad associations—will usually suffer the most. They may very well grow up never having been corrected for the way they're relating to others. As a result, they won't be popular or effective in dealing with other people as they get older. And they'll probably find that their own self-confidence begins to suffer as they mature.

Usually, there's little you can do to help such children, even if you know their parents very well. Most parents resent intervention or unsolicited advice in their own child rearing. We all tend to develop blind spots in our attempts to bring up our children properly.

So even as you limit your child's association with certain children, you should also watch carefully to be certain that *your* child is not the one who is creating the problems. An ability to work with other people is one of the most important ingredients in success in later life; and it's a skill that children begin to develop at a very early age. As a result, it's very important to pay close attention to exactly how your toddler is interacting with other children.

Tip #3: Let Your Child Test His Environment in Minute Detail

One of the irritations that the "terrible twos" inflict on their parents is to try to test out many things that are told to them. Instead of automatically accepting what's communicated to them, they want to check for themselves.

My Bonnie loves soft drinks, and whenever we had them when she was a toddler, she always wanted to be sure that the can was completely empty. I'd tell her it was indeed empty, but she would insist, "Me check."

Then, she'd shake the can, and, of course, there was usually a tiny bit of soda in the bottom.

"Little bit, Mommy!" she'd say triumphantly, obviously feeling happy that she'd proved me wrong.

A little nettling to me, I'll have to admit. But her attentiveness was also encouraging. It was an indication that Bonnie was developing the self-confidence to find things out for herself—not just to accept meekly everything that was told to her by adults.

I believe that a child's resolute insistence on checking even the most minute details of a current interest deserves your respect and undivided attention when that's possible. Sometimes—in fact, most times—that will demand a certain amount of one-to-one communication.

For this reason among others, I oppose nursery-school rearing for very small children. Even the cleverest teacher will find it almost impossible to deal with the concern of one toddler for detail and at the same time manage the entire class. Anyone who is attempting to watch five, six, seven or more children can't be expected to concentrate perceptively on the questions that one particular child is asking, especially if those questions seem irrelevant to the main topic under consideration.

But, unfortunately, when you ignore a child's challenge to your statements or fail to provide him with an opportunity to test what you've told him, you instill bad habits in him. What exactly are these? For one thing, you'll encourage sloppy thinking and inattention to detail, deficiencies that will surface in later childhood in a number of ways. The child may become timid or hesitant about challenging the assertion of others. Or he may simply become uninterested in personally checking out facts that are communicated to him.

Certainly, if a day-school teacher *or* a tired or distracted parent consistently reacts angrily when a child makes what seem like carping or distrustful observations, the youngster will be discouraged from making further observations. By indicating to him that you're displeased with or uninterested in his concerns, you'll unintentionally begin to whittle away at his self-confidence. As a consequence, he'll be less inclined to form and assert his own opinions.

One mother I know would wash her kitchen sink frequently in her toddler daughter's presence. The little girl was especially fascinated by the bubbles created by the cleanser and would continually ask during the cleaning process, "Bubbles all gone, Mommy?"

The mother would have to report regularly to her, "Almost gone," or perhaps, "One or two bubbles left."

The daughter would nod approvingly at this information, but she wasn't always satisfied with her mother's report. Instead, she would want to check it out for herself: "Lemme see!" she'd often say.

It was easy to laugh about these childish concerns—just as long as the mother was not rushed or under pressure. But when Mom began to feel overwhelmed by all the things she had to get done in a given day, she'd sometimes get annoyed. In irritation she'd tend to dismiss the incessant questioning with a blanket statement. In fact, sometimes it was all she could do to restrain herself from snapping, "Shut up! Go play while I do my work!"

This temptation to vent frustration becomes infinitely greater for the mother who suffers from what I call a "state of depletion." This is a condition of physical or emotional exhaustion that makes it practically impossible to deal with a pressing, omnipresent toddler on a completely rational basis.

When you begin to feel that you're going to be pushed over the edge, it's important to take a deep breath, step back and get perspective on the situation. Obviously, none of us is perfect; we're occasionally going to lash out or be unfair. But I'm also convinced that the inclination and ability of a child to push, explore and make fine distinctions is crucial for later success in life.

The ability to access accurately the world around you and determine just how you fit into the scheme of things is extremely important. Also, the determination to be *precise* is essential to achievement and excellence in a variety of fields, including languages and mathematics.

So restrain yourself from flying off the handle when your child seems to be holding onto an issue like a little bulldog. Remember the skills that he's developing, even as he's exasperating you. The minor annoyances that you may be experiencing now will be far outweighed by the later benefits to your child's sense of inner assurance.

Tip #4: Avoid Significant Separations from Your Toddler

Before a child reaches age three, he's especially vulnerable to emotional problems that may be compounded by separation from his primary caretaker. An intimate involvement and interplay between mother and child is critical during this period.

Why is this? For one thing, your child is already beginning to cope with an early form of "separation anxiety": He has a growing realization that he's no longer the only important element in his environment. Also, he begins to understand that his safety and well-being are highly dependent on the primary caretaker. Consequently, it's risky to add physical separation to this growing sense of uncertainty.

But does this mean that the mother should never get away, that she should never have a "Mom's day out?" Certainly not!

To keep your sanity, you *have* to find relief from the constant presence of your child. No matter how much you love her, you won't be able to deal with her questions, comments, observations and bad moods with freshness and creativity unless you yourself are well rested. As a result, I believe that a judicious use of baby-sitters, Sunday school classes, play dates or other limited outings for the child—where the mother doesn't have to be involved—are essential.

At the same time, I would avoid *lengthy* absences from your child during this toddler stage—such as a vacation. For some families, it may work for the parents to spend a week or two away from their children. But there should be exciting, attractive—and attentive—alternative caretakers for the children, such as loving grandparents or other relatives. In any case, if the child's attitude towards the alternative caretaker seems to involve more anxiety than excitement, I would be reluctant to plan that separate vacation.

Tip #5: But Togetherness with Your Toddler Doesn't Mean Returning to the Womb!

Some moves toward independence may be painful for the toddler, but they should be encouraged for the sake of all involved.

One good example is the resistance that most children have to bedtime. A related problem is their tendency to want to crawl into bed regularly with Mom and Dad.

Consider this touching paragraph from a leading family magazine:

> For thousands of American kids, every night is the loneliest night of the week, come nine P.M. when their happy, loving families turn abruptly into untouchables. Junior is sent to his lonely bed space . . . There are few sights sadder than the thin back of a child as he goes off to face the night alone.

This article was promoting a kind of family-sleep-together movement, and I must say I can identify with some of the sentiments expressed. It *is* difficult to turn your back on your son and daughter when they're crying, "But Mommy, I just want one last kiss!"

Still, when you consider that you may have bestowed a dozen kisses before that "final" one, the youthful request begins to look a little less reasonable. Yet either by design or accident, many parents fall into the trap of allowing their toddlers and even much older children to crawl into bed with them.

Now, I'm not saying that parents should *never* allow their youngsters to join them for a warm cuddle and snooze. But if you've had any experience with toddlers and other very young children, you'll know that one entrée into the master bedroom will inevitably lead to another and still another—until finally, the parents' boudoir has become an extension of the childrens' bedroom.

That result, I believe, is ultimately neither desirable nor even healthy. As one psychologist who has worked with families for many years comments, "Not once have I talked with parents who are satisfied with the arrangement."

The main point here is that the general movement of your children during toddlerhood should be toward spending the entire night by themselves in their own rooms. Certainly, there may be extenuating circumstances, especially if a child is having a bad night or seems otherwise in need of extra parental comfort and communication.

But if you find that your child is spending more and more time in bed with you, that may be a signal that instead of heading toward a healthy independence, he's moving in the opposite direction: He may be retreating toward the womb, rather than developing a secure, forceful inner self.

Tip #6: Encourage Your Toddler To Be His Own Little Person

Also perilous to youngsters in their terrible twos phase are over-ambitious parents who may try to push them to conform to a preconceived role model.

That model may be one that the parents have never achieved, or it may be one created by a successful older sibling. Whatever the source, when such role models are forced on a youngster with little regard for his own abilities and interests, the result will be damaging to his self-concept.

To understand how frustrating this can be for a youngster, try putting yourself in his shoes. There are certain things you like and others you dislike. But suppose someone more powerful than you said you can't do what you like, and you have to do what you dislike. Furthermore, you must pretend that you like it!

Not a very pleasant prospect, is it? In fact, it can be truly horrifying when the most important people in your small world begin to push you in a direction you don't like. And then they regularly show their disappointment over your inadequate efforts to please them.

So back off! Allow your child to develop in his own way. Be sensitive to what his strengths and weaknesses are and how you can help him become the person that he's meant to be.

"Tip #7: Avoid "Zingers"

Some overly ambitious parents unconsciously attack their child's basic self-confidence in yet another way: They seem unable to prasie him without appending some negative or derogatory comment.

Search your soul here: How many times have you been guilty of this very thing? How quick are you to point out to your offspring where he has failed or committed some wrong?

One thing that I suggest parents do is to take an average day—perhaps today or yesterday—and total up the number of times that they've resorted to negative "zingers" in interactions with their children. For all but the very best of parents, the result is usually dismaying. For most of us, such confidence-sapping criticisms far outnumber the expressions of praise we offer our child for something he or she has done well or right.

When you deal with adults who add zingers to their remarks, you know what an ego-dampening impact their negative criticism can have on you. If you're smart, you avoid such people like the plague.

But your little child can't avoid Mom or Dad. For better or worse, he's *married* to his parents. Not only are the mother and father in effect gods in the toddler's world; they can also play the part of a disapproving deity who is forever finding fault.

Of course, toddlers have not developed the language skills to be able to understand everything you say to them. But they certainly get the general message—especially *negative* messages—from your tone of voice, body posture and that stern look in your eye.

One father I know had a problem with his two-and-a-half-year-old who kept insisting on marking up the walls of his room with crayons.

When the little boy finally got through a day without committing this domestic crime, the father praised him by saying, "That's great, Teddy. You did just the right thing today by staying away from your walls. Look how clean they are!"

But then he added reproachfully, "Why can't you be like this all the time? You make us so unhappy when you misbehave."

Teddy didn't react visibly to this zinger. But I can't help feeling that a series of remarks like this, beginning in toddlerhood, are going to ingrain a negative message in a child's mind: "Yes, you do some things that we're proud of. But in general, you just don't make the grade. You don't cut the mustard. You don't do quite enough of what you're supposed to do."

Unfortunately, zingers tend to be a regular part of the vocabulary in most parents. Here are some typical examples that I have come across in my own work.

- One little boy had just learned to tie his shoelaces, but he became so absorbed in the process that he failed to notice that he had put his sneakers on the wrong feet. Proudly, he walked over to his father to get some praise for his accomplishment.

  "That's great, you really did a good job!" Dad said. "But look what you did—you got your shoes on the wrong feet!"

  Embarassed, the youngster went back to untie his shoelaces and switch his shoes around. Obviously, the triumph that he might have felt in his achievement had been seriously undercut by the zinger that his dad had attached to the compliment.
- An elementary school child labored long and hard over a short story that she had written on her own. She didn't know how to spell many of the words she was using, but she did know the point she wanted to get across, and on the whole, she did an excellent, rather precocious, job of achieving her goal.

  But then, when she went to show her mother the three pages that she had written, the parent focused on the mispelled words and the handwriting that in some cases was rather messy. To be sure, the mother did compliment her daughter for doing a good job in conceptualizing the story. But the qualifications and negatives that she had attached to her encouragement certainly did little to foster a sense of self-confidence in this youngster.
- A little boy who loved to sing was performing in a Sunday school choral group. The songs were executed quite well, and

this youngster contributed a great deal to the high quality of the performance. But during the songs, he twisted his face and nose around, apparently because he was nervous at appearing before an audience.

After the performance was finished and compliments and accolades were being passed out by parents and the music director during the refreshment time, the boy's father pulled his son aside and said, ''You did a nice job up there, but in the future, try not to make faces while you're singing. That distracts from the music.''

The boy, thoroughly deflated, lost much of the reinforcement that he had received toward a more positive self-image.

When a child does something well, we, in typical adult fashion, promptly think about how he or she could have done it better. Or we compare the achievement to some poor past performance. We use what should be an occasion for congratulation as an opportunity to sermonize. We deplore yesterday's lapse or exhort the child to do better tomorrow.

So can you blame your youngster for feeling discouraged? Is it surprising if he gets a little bit rebellious when he simply can't seem to win your unconditional approval.

So next time you praise your child, watch what you say. If you rid yourself of the habit of throwing out those zingers when your child is quite young, you'll likely set a pattern for you as well as for him well into the future.

Tip #8: Help Your Toddler To Become Decisive

A major phase in terrible-two development is the child's struggle to make decisions for himself. The parents' approach to decision making can either fortify a youngster's self-confidence or badly undercut it.

To fortify self-confidence, I'd suggest one *do* and one *don't*:

- *Do* give your child simple choices, when it's necessary for her to make decisions involving comparisons.

One mother told her daughter, "Pick out a shirt from your drawer—one that you'd like to wear today." That's asking too much of a two- or three-year-old. The many choices that are available in such a request are likely to be overwhelming, simply because there will probably be too many shirts to choose from.

Instead, this mother should have preselected two acceptable shirts and *then* asked, "Which one would you like to wear?" With the possible choices thus narrowed down, the toddler could confidently decide which one she liked and feel proud that she had contributed significantly to her daily ritual of dressing.

That's the way the "Do" works. Now for the "Don't."

• *Don't* place yourself in the position of eliciting a response that you know you'll have to overrule.

If you want to teach your child how to make decisions and gain confidence in voicing opinions, don't set him up so that only one answer will be right. In other words, don't cause his response in effect to become irrelevant.

For example, it was time for one mother and her two-and-a-half-year-old daughter to leave the playground because the mother had another engagement. In addition, the playground facility was just about to close. So it was futile—in fact, stupid!—for the mother to ask, as she did, "Would you like to leave now?"

Predictably, the daughter responded, "No, no! I want to stay!"

The mother thus found that she was unable to honor the very choice she had offered. Fortunately, this mother learned at an early point that this was not the right way to approach decision making. Following some advice from a wiser source, she came up with another alternative that was much better. It worked this way:

Five to ten minutes before they actually had to leave, the mother asked, "Are you ready to go now, Susie? It's getting late, and we really should go."

As might be expected, Susie replied, "No, Mommy, No!"

Then, the mother replied, "Well, all right, we can stay for just a little while longer if you like."

In this way, the mother avoided summarily overruling her toddler. In addition, she allowed the little girl some input in the final decision. Finally, by giving advance notice that they would have to leave before long, the mother avoided having to drag the girl screaming from the playground.

Of course, parents can't always rely on diplomacy. You may give your youngster notice and still encounter resistance when it's time to act. Or you may forget to prepare the child for the inevitable and end up unable to take no for an answer.

In such situations, it's best not to ask your child to make a decision. For example, if it's her bedtime, you shouldn't ask your child, "Are you sleepy? Do you want to go bye-bye?"

With this sort of query you risk a resounding "No!" Instead, mother or father should say firmly, "Off to bed, young lady!" and should be prepared to back up that statement with discipline if necessary.

It's always best to avoid confrontations with children, but sometimes that's just not possible. When rational discussion or opportunities for the children to make decisions are impossible, the next best thing is to be straightforward and unequivocal. It's much less confusing to the youngster to operate this way than to solicit an opinion and then promptly overrule it.

As your child advances to age three, he'll become more and more verbal. During this phase, the crude forms of communication you've adopted up to this point will blossom into full-blown discussions. The result can be increased enjoyment and excitement in the family—but also increased opportunities for conflict.

As your child's language abilities improve, you'll find that you have to combine the patience of Job with the tact of a professional diplomat—not to mention the occasional disciplinary firmness of a Marine drill sergeant. Throughout it all, the major objective that must always be before you is to relate to your child in a way that will bolster her sense of identity and nurture in her the seeds of self-confidence.

A staggering order, to be sure. But it's achievable, so long as you learn some of the subtleties of what I call "self-confident talk."

5

Self-Confident Talk

"**S**elf-confident talk" builds inner assurance in the child by focusing on those words, phrases and responses that will build up the child's self-esteem. This special language becomes extremely important when the child finds himself in difficult, threatening situations.

As a simple illustration, consider a typical accident involving a toddler who is just beginning to develop his fine motor skills. My Bonnie once picked a dish off the kitchen table on her own initiative and proceeded to drop and shatter it on the floor. Without thinking, I snapped, "That sure was clumsy, Bonnie! You're always getting into things you're not supposed to!"

That's telling her, I thought; that's teaching her not to mess around with my precious china!

Unfortunately, I was also conveying an underlying message that tended to make Bonnie feel worthless and inadequate. With too many such parental outbursts, she would begin to assume, "I'm clumsy. I'm always doing the wrong thing."

What's the right reaction to such childish accidents? In that situation I should have said—and did finally learn to say—"Oh, dear, you dropped the dish. But that's all right. You're just not quite ready yet to handle big dishes. But very soon you will be, and I'll be so proud of you. For now, though, let's let Mommy take care of dishes on the table, all right?"

Agreed, this calls for almost saintly self-restraint. And I must

71

admit that I haven't always been up to such a response. But in terms of a child's fragile, developing ego, it's worth the effort to use this kind of communication.

Obviously, if you respond to your child this way and then she proceeds almost immediately to pick up another dish and drop it, you've moved into another dimension of parent-child interaction. Now, she's not trying to explore and develop new skills. Rather, she's probably being defiant or disobedient. And that will call for some sort of reprimand or disciplinary action.

But the first time around, it's best to go easy and use some form of self-confident talk to get your point across.

What are some of the basic principles to keep in mind when you're trying to engage in self-confident talk with your child? Here are a few.

- Don't overload encouragement and compliments with instruction. Sometimes, parents may conscientiously avoid including negative zingers in their conversation, but they may still overdo it when it comes to pressing their children to improve their performance in various areas of life. On the whole, I think encouraging, edifying comments and conversations with children do a great deal more than a steady stream of "teaching" on a variety of subjects.
- Choose words and phrases that tend to build your youngster up rather than tear him down. Sometimes you may think that what you're saying is entirely innocent and in fact said jokingly or in good humor. You may say, "Come on, Johnny, you may turn into a dog if you keep swimming that dog paddle. Try getting your hands out of the water and doing a crawl!" Such a comment might evoke laughter, but if your child thinks the laughter is at *his* expense, it may very well do more harm than good in improving his self-image.
- Emphasize "can do" language. For example, you might say, "You can learn to ride that bike if you'll just keep trying! I *know* you can!" Telling a child that an achievement is within his grasp may be all that he needs to pursue an achieve his goal.
- Encourage your child to emphasize the positive rather than the negative in her own conversations about herself and others. I know one little girl who has been so well trained in this regard that when she hears her mother say something downbeat or

negative about herself or someone else, she'll exclaim, "Mommy, you're a negative thinker!"

- Don't confuse self-confident talk by your child with sassiness, disrespect or boastfulness. There's a fine line between being upbeat and being overbearing or obnoxious. Yet it's easy for young children to cross that line before they've had a chance to develop a full measure of judgment.

USING SELF-CONFIDENT COMMUNICATION

Now, let's consider a few examples of the right way and the wrong way to handle some annoying, embarrassing or awkward situations that toddlers are so skilled at creating. In every situation, the parent can score a point for the child's inner security by using some type of self-confident communication.

Uncle Bob the Slob

At some point between the ages of two and three, most children find they have the opportunity to reprimand some adult for not following family rules of good conduct.

One woman I know had been very careful in teaching her three-year-old boy *not* to put his feet up on the coffee table. In fact, this offense was one of the few the family found unforgivable, and it resulted in immediate disciplinary action when it occurred.

As it happened, the mother had laid down this rule because she detested the fact that one of the family's relatives, Uncle Bob, was often guilty of that rather uncouth practice. But then the predictable occurred. Uncle Bob came to visit one day and did just what the woman of the house had prohibited the child from doing: He put his big, dirty feet up on the coffee table. The toddler immediately snapped, "In our house, *we don't put our feet on the table!*"

The words, and even the scolding tone, were precisely those the mother always used with the child. Uncle Bob, a bachelor unaccustomed to dealing with children, took offense, even though his antagonist was only a three-year-old boy. The mother, sensitive to

Bob's discomfort, turned to her son and said, "Honey, don't say that to Uncle Bob!"

What a devastating situation for the little boy! He felt that somehow he had done something wrong in merely repeating what his mother often had—that you don't put your feet on the table. He left the room confused, embarrassed and even humiliated by the scolding.

Also, it's likely that this child learned something about the inconsistency of adults in dealing with each other and in promoting and following social and moral principles. The confusion and uncertainty undoubtedly helped to weaken this little boy's budding self-confidence, at least to some degree.

Sooner or later, all children must learn to deal with the double standard that holds certain behaviors unacceptable in children but acceptable or forgivable in adults!

Such a concept is too subtle for a toddler. At that age everything is black or white. Consequently, unless the parent can inject some powerful self-confident talk to explain the situation, the child's inner being will be shaken.

What should the mother have said in this case?

Something like this: "That's right, dear. We don't put our feet on the table. And I'm so glad that you remembered the rule."

This would have strengthened, rather than weakened, her son's sense of what was right. And what about Uncle Bob? He would have been miffed no matter what the mother had said. But I'm also sure that he would never again have put his feet on the table in that home!

Little Miss Bossy

One three-and-a-half-year-old girl found herself in a strange, actually frightening situation. Her family had recently moved to a new city, and she was trying to adjust to the alien surroundings. To make things worse, her mother was preparing to return to work—a factor that added to the youngster's uneasiness.

Like many children faced with such threats to a previously secure world, she became bossy. She would echo her mother's orders to her when she met relatives or other children. In general, she behaved like a miniature drill sergeant when dealing with the outside world.

In some ways, this was a healthy and quite effective way of enabling her to cope with a series of uncertainties in her life. In effect, she was saying subconsciously to herself, "I'm going to try to control everything I can because there are so many things I can't control. I've just *got* to get hold of some things in my life!"

This was fine, so long as she was around plenty of supportive people who understood what she was going through. But then trouble entered in the form of Grandpa, who decided to make his first visit to the family in more than a year.

He pictured himself as a Norman Rockwell character, holding his little granddaughter in his lap while she happily—and respectfully—listened to his stories. He was totally unprepared to be henpecked and bossed around by a virtual baby!

This was all the homemade TNT you'd need for a family explosion, and sure enough, Grandpa's visit ended in disaster. The little girl refused to kowtow to him on many issues. She even reprimanded him several times for disagreeing with her! As a result, he ended his visit before he had planned, in a complete huff. To put the finishing touch to a bad situation, the child dissolved in tears when her mother upbraided her for driving the old man away.

In this particular situation, the father turned out to be the hero. When he arrived home from work on the same day that Grandpa had walked out, he was able to evaluate the situation with considerably more objectivity than his wife.

In a private conversation with his spouse, he pointed out that their daughter had been reacting in a predictable, if not entirely respectful or acceptable, way. Finally, the mother began to understand more fully that the girl's behavior, though exasperating, was understandable at her stage of development.

The woman also acknowledged that Grandpa should have been briefed well in advance about his granddaughter's problems so that he would have had some opportunity to prepare for what was coming. The parents' lack of foresight had been an additional cause in the often inevitable collision between youth and age.

Fortunately, this mother was sensitive and intelligent enough to realize what had happened. She also knew what she had to do to set things right.

She went to her daughter and said, "I love you very much, and I know you're going through a tough time right now, with our family move and everything. I should have told Grandpa about what we've been going through, and also, I should have told you about what to expect from him. The next time, we'll all try to understand each other a little better, okay? In the meantime, why don't we write Grandpa a letter, tell him we're sorry and invite him back in a few months?"

The daughter readily agreed, and she was able to put her tiff with her grandfather in perspective. Soon, the situation in the household was back on the right track.

Obviously, the situation had other ramifications. The little girl had gone too far with her grandfather, and at some point it would be necessary for her parents to help her overcome the deficiencies in her conduct.

But for the present, it was much more important for the parents to let the daughter know that she was loved and accepted, even if she had overstepped herself.

The Doctor's Office

Most parents lie to their children at some time, but this prevalence doesn't make lying excusable. Morality aside, lying is largely self-defeating.

In the first place, you'll find it quite difficult to fool a reasonably intelligent child, especially after you've attempted to once or twice. And once your duplicity is exposed, your child will be far less likely to trust you—and, by extension, himself. After all, who *can* feel confident in a world filled with lies and deception?

A classic example of the "innocent," often inadvertent parental lie is telling the child who must face the doctor's needle, "It won't hurt." Granted, many modern doctors reduce the pain in such situations with special solutions that deaden the outer skin, but there's no question about it; sometimes shots do hurt.

So it's really rather stupid to say, "This won't hurt," when obviously that's not true. And it *really* rubs the child's nose in the lie when you say after the shot's administered, "Now that didn't hurt, did it?"

Of course it did! Moreover, you've once again made your child a little less trusting of you—and probably less confident in his own feelings.

In short, it's important when a child begins to go for regular doctor's or dentist's checkups, that you prepare him with the right kind of self-confident talk. First, consider situations that involve giving children unpleasant-tasting medicines, or treating them for painful cuts or bruises, or subjecting them to medical experiences that will be, at best, unpleasant. It's best to say something like this:

"Yes, you'll feel a little sting, but if you'll count up to three after I put this on, it'll all be over."

This approach acknowledges the fact that the antiseptic or whatever it is you're applying won't feel very nice, but at the same time, it lets the child know that the mild pain will be ending very quickly. You can make a statement like this very honestly and reassure the child that he'll emerge intact on the other side of the experience.

Of course, none of this means that you're going to get away without tears or resistance in every case. But at least you'll be providing your youngster with a firm emotional foundation to deal with some of the pain and unpleasantness he's bound to face in his life.

In more serious cases—for example, where your youngster may have to be hospitalized—most larger institutions will provide dolls that have been made to represent the same illness as the one suffered by the child. With these toys, the youngster can work out some of his anxiety by playing "doctor" to the doll. This way, he turns his passive hospital role into a more active, healing role with the doll. Such directed play seems to diffuse much of a youngster's anxiety and anger over being so helpless. Also, this technique helps to give him a greater sense of self-control and self-confidence.

In one hospital where I worked, there were also booklets by "Mister Rogers" and others directed to both parents and children on what to expect in the hospital. If you look hard enough and think seriously about ways that you can communicate to your child how best to deal with his problem, you'll certainly find plenty of ways to inject self-confident talk into each situation.

Finally, one of the most traumatic, confidence-shaking experiences for a toddler in the health area may involve a trip to the dentist.

These days, many dentists consult in advance with parents of youngsters who must undergo painful procedures. Sometimes, before they are to be worked on, the little patients are shown the tools that are going to be used in treating them. With young children, this kind of orientation seems to make a big difference. It doesn't mean that they'll enjoy the experience—just that they'll have more information and resources with which to dispell their fears.

The old-fashioned approach was not to warn children of an upcoming unpleasant experience. The reasoning was that you could minimize the effects of a problem by not anticipating it—and there is a grain of truth in this. It's been shown by a number of studies that the most painful part of many experiences lies in anticipating them.

But for children facing serious medical difficulties, and especially work in the dentist's chair, this approach is about 180 degrees wrong. *Cruelly* wrong.

The sudden shock of a tooth extraction, for example, or an operation that has to be performed without any advance explanation, can cause a tremendous emotional upheaval. A youngster's basic trust in his environment and the people around him will be badly shaken.

Conversely, when a child believes his feelings are being respected, he'll have a greater sense of control. He may even try to help the doctor execute the procedure smoothly.

I've watched the technique of sensitive orthopedists as they unwrap gauze around a child's leg to check the healing of a fracture. All the while, they encourage the youngster, who may be as young as age three, to help hold the gauze and inspect the medicine that's being painted on the injured leg. Often, some of the medicine gets daubed on the doll, or even the doctor.

But even though things can get a little messy with this approach, it amazes me how quiet and cooperative such children become. Their behavior is particularly striking when you compare them with those whose bodies are simply *invaded* by the physician. The former develop confidence in the ability and intention of the adult to help them; the latter become panicked by feelings of helplessness.

The plight of the sick child is little different from that of the sick adult. In both cases, the individual may be overwhelmed by a problem that is not of his doing and beyond his control. Even the strongest adults may feel that they are helpless, and their self-confidence may be severely affected. But once they begin to believe that they can participate in the healing or rebuilding process, their sense of integrity and self-confidence can be restored.

This same coping technique can become part of the coping arsenal of a sick child, especially when he is being treated sensitively.

The Social Contretemps

Most of us have been in this position or one similar to it many times: You're visiting someone whom you don't know very well, and suddenly your child blurts out, "I want to go home!"

Unfortunately, he doesn't stop there. He gets embarrassingly specific, as he explains that he wants to go home because he's tired, or hungry, or bored or—worst of all—he just doesn't like the hostess' house.

Your natural response, in trying to diffuse an awkward situation, is to counter, "You don't mean that!"

But of course he means it. Better than anyone else, he knows when he's hungry, tired or bored. Your knee-jerk response only confuses him because he's learned to treat everything you say with some respect. He may not agree with you all the time, but at least he knows that you and your opinions are something to be reckoned with. Now, however, you've denied what he *knows* he feels.

Any wonder that he may be confused? And confusion will almost always lead to self-doubt.

But there's more to it than this. On another level, you're really lying to him when you say, "You don't mean that!" or "You're not hungry!"

You may think, well, I wasn't really lying; I was just trying to be polite. But small children are not that sophisticated or subtle. Even the little white lies that may be part of what we call good manners are not easy for them to distinguish from the whoppers. Children are the world's greatest truth tellers, and we shouldn't want them to be otherwise. So when you say, "You don't mean that!" you're putting your child in a very difficult position.

What should you do?

It's best to be as straightforward in such circumstances as your child is being with you. Perhaps you might tell him that he'll have to wait until you're ready to go before he can eat, or whatever it is he wants to do. Or if he is hungry, you might ask your hostess for a cracker or cookie for him. Above all, acknowledge the validity of what he is saying. Treat his complaint with respect, and don't pretend that a fact is not a fact.

When you stop to think about it, social or personal encounters entailing subtle distinctions between truth and falsehood may have the same effects on adults as they have on children. Furthermore, many of the things that undermine a child's self-confidence are no different from those that undermine self-confidence in an adult.

Suppose you're a boss with a new secretary who is trying desperately to become competent at her job. But her problem is that she doesn't yet know the ropes in the office or in the industry. She can't always distinguish between the subtleties of various relationships or business deals.

You, of course, know your business and the customs of the marketplace backwards and forwards. So you proceed to communicate with her on the level that you're used to. From her point of view, however, you are simply being confusing.

For example, one day the phone calls she puts through to you from a certain person are fine. The next day, you reprimand her for bothering you with them. What's right and what's wrong in this situation? She's too new on the job to figure out your system without considerable explanation. Yet you're in a hurry to get the job done. Unfortunately, when you move too fast or make things too complicated for her, and then upbraid her for not understanding, you'll shake her self-confidence badly.

If this dynamic is true in the case of reasonably intelligent, mature adults, how much more true is it for unsophisticated, literal-minded children! So try to tune in more to the way your child thinks and reacts in unfamiliar social situations. Deal with him more on his level than on yours. That way, you'll avoid the prospect of an unpleasant contretemp and also pave the way for his feelings of security when he's confronted by more subtle challenges in the future.

Is It Really Rudeness?

I have a friend who is constantly embarrassed by the "rude" reaction of her three-year-old son toward a female neighbor. The neighbor, who has had very little experience with small children, takes it personally because the child refuses to run up to her, throw his arms about her and kiss her.

Worse than that, because the toddler is going through a major contrary phase, he's more apt to say, "Get away, I hate you," when she attempts to hug him.

A rather unsociable attitude—but still quite understandable. In addition to being predisposed to contrariness, this boy senses that his environment is being invaded by an outsider. He has not yet developed the kind of subtle defenses employed by adults when their turf is encroached upon. So he blasts her with a verbal assault.

As grown-ups, we often practice what I call "pseudo intimacy" in many situations involving strangers. In other words, we may "appear" to be friendly and gregarious, even though we often couldn't care less about the person we're talking to. We may even dislike that person actively!

A small child is incapable of such playacting. When he feels threatened, he becomes angry and pulls away from those well-meaning people who may want to hug and kiss him.

My daughter, Bonnie, when confronted by a stranger during those toddler years, would hide behind my skirts. She wouldn't allow unknown people to invade her space.

What's the answer to this problem?

First of all, in the child's own time and on her own terms, she will begin to get more "sociable." Furthermore, the most effective self-confident talk in this situation is communication that gives the child a little room to maneuver. If you try to push a youngster into certain actions that aren't appropriate to her developmental stage, you'll only confuse her. And as we've seen, confusion leads, in the long run, to weakened self-confidence.

Of course, even when a child is deep into this negative and contrary phase of his development, it's still important to keep his behavior reasonably socially acceptable. In other words, things should rarely get to the point where he is forced to say, "I hate you!"

If you'll just understand what's behind the apparent "rudeness" your child is demonstrating, you'll probably come to accept the fact that there's a good reason for it, at least from his point of view. He's trying to tell you something by being shy, reclusive or reserved. If you try to tell him it's wrong for him to feel that way, he may very well lash out and embarrass you.

On the other hand, if you try talking with him more reassuringly and explore together what's behind his reluctance, you'll assist him much more meaningfully in this part of the growing-up process.

On Getting Dressed

I can think of no more time consuming, and many times annoying, maternal chore than teaching a child to dress himself. In many cases, the youngster doesn't want to sacrifice the comfort and security of having Mom dress him. Also, it's boring and distracting to have to pull on those pants, socks, shirt and shoes when you'd really rather be playing with some toy while someone else puts your clothes on you. So he resists learning to do it on his own.

Even after he reaches that magic day when he begins to link dressing himself with being grown up, there can be plenty of problems in streamlining the process. One of the greatest difficulties for some children is distinguishing the front of an undershirt from the back. Such tasks can provide good occasions for some highly effective parental self-confident talk.

I know one mother whose son came to her flushed with pride about a recent accomplishment with his clothes. He said triumphantly, "Mommy, I got dressed all by myself. And I got everything on right this time."

Of course, the undershirt was on backwards. So what's a mom to do? In this case, the mom praised the boy for having performed the chore all by himself. But then, she felt impelled to add, "Well, honey, actually everything is right except the undershirt. It's on backwards."

With this observation, all the boy's pride in his accomplishment went right down the tubes. He felt crushed. The mother immediately sensed that she had let the boy down badly, but she didn't quite grasp exactly how she had gone wrong.

Her error was in failing to recognize the overriding principle that was involved, the thing that was *really* important in this situation. This was that the boy had performed the job by himself. Also, he was making a great effort to try to correct earlier mistakes of getting his clothes on wrong.

So what should the mother have done in this case?

Suppose she had let him wear the undershirt incorrectly? There would have been absolutely no problem! Then, after she had waited for the moment to pass and his pride in his accomplishment had become firmly fixed, she might have instructed him about how to look for the label on the shirt and be sure it was at his back when he put it on.

In short, the proper self-confident talk in this situation might have been, first of all, not to talk at all. Just wait a few moments so that the boy's confidence could have become more fixed. Then, at a later time, she could have taught him the right way.

Don't Argue

As your child begins to test his control of the world and stretch his burgeoning language abilities, he'll sometimes waver between likes and dislikes in ways that can be most exasperating to any parent.

So, one morning your daughter may push away her cereal, even though she gobbled it all up the previous morning. Then, the next day she may like it again. When you notice this inconsistency, there's no point in making a big issue out of it.

You can certainly raise the question: "What's the matter— something wrong with the cereal? You ate it all up yesterday."

But if her response is negative I wouldn't push the subject too hard. If there's one thing I've learned about toddlers, it's this: It doesn't pay to argue over a small child's transient feelings. You'll just waste your time. The only effect you'll have on her—if you have any effect at all—is to push her into a cranky mood.

Toddlers who are just experimenting with many aspects of their world simply don't act like little adults. In fact, they're *not* little adults! It's important to keep in mind that even though your three-year-old may be developing a pretty good command of simple verbal skills, he may still not think in the same reasonable, logical terms that you do. (If you think about it, many *adults* don't think in such reasonable, logical terms either!)

Of course, I'm not suggesting that we can create a perfect world at home where there are never any arguments. Granted, it's a great idea to *work* toward that ideal of peaceful, low-key conversations between parents and children, but, obviously, there are going to be eruptions and arguments that will break out in every home at one time or another.

The main point that I want to make here is that a toddler is not capable of engaging in a rational, head-to-head debate with a parent on any issue. Although the youngster's verbal skills may be great, they're not good enough to deal with the power and subtlety of adult expression. Most likely, you'll only succeed in backing your child into a corner and causing him to respond stubbornly to your attack. He won't learn anything about engaging in verbal repartee. He'll just learn techniques of "getting his back up," or "stonewalling" to head off a more powerful verbal onslaught.

Most important of all, none of this will do a thing to enhance his self-confidence. In fact, the most effective self-confident talk *never* includes arguments. You'll have to *tell* your child what to do sometimes, no doubt about that. But that's an entirely different subject. The real power of self-confident talk rests in the ability of the parent to use reassuring and often subtle language to help a child learn to think and do the right things on his own.

The experience of moving through toddlerhood can be as much a challenge for the serious parent as for the child. But if you'll take pains to lay the right groundwork at this stage, you'll find that many problems can be avoided in later stages of development. Furthermore, the ability of the child to be self-confident will grow steadily upon these early foundations that you've worked so hard to build.

6

Crisis Three: The Sibling Salvos

When one child is operating by himself in the family, with only his mother and father as reference points, he will encounter plenty of challenges to his developing self-confidence. But when another child comes along, those challenges increase considerably.

In short, questions and difficulties multiply for children *and* parents when siblings are added to the family. These additional issues involve what I call the "multiplier factor."

THE MULTIPLIER FACTOR

As we begin to explore the rivalries and interactions that arise among siblings, a host of issues confront us. For example:

- How do you combat potentially destructive forces that pit older and younger children against each other?
- What supportive measures should you take to strengthen the self-confidence of all your youngsters?
- How should you respond if one of your youngsters, in the throes of sibling conflict, displays a need for a "security blanket"?
- Will long-term breast-feeding help foster dependence or independence among siblings?

- What special self-confidence problems are likely to be encountered by your older and younger children?

Actually, perhaps the first question that should be asked is, "What does the arrival of a second child do to the *parents'* self-confidence and sense of well-being?"

In this regard, one pundit has observed in the *New York Times*, "one child plus one child equals *more* than two times the food eaten, clothes dirtied, rooms left untidied, calls for mommy, cries for daddy, bruises tended, car pools driven."

In other words, for many parents it's a lot tougher to have two children than it is to have one. One mother has observed, "Nothing prepares you for the reality of two. Two means more than twice the work and less than half the time and energy to do it."

In some ways, this view makes a lot of sense. Although many parents would argue that having two children gives parents more time because the first child now has a playmate, the reality is not quite so simple. To be sure, children who are fairly close together in age will be able to play together. But they will also be able to *fight* together—and that means a parent usually has to intervene to settle disputes.

Also, just adding one additional personality multiplies the number of variations for interpersonal contact and conflict in a family. Some child-rearing experts have distinguished between the one- and two-child families by saying that having one child is "reversible." In other words, after the first two or three years in an only-child family, the parents can resume their careers and social activities on a relatively normal basis.

But two children tend to require a more serious commitment on the part of both adults to the concept of "family." Among other things, this means the ideals of self-realization for each spouse must take a back seat.

As difficult as it can be for the parents to adjust to the presence of a second child, it can be infinitely more confidence-shaking for the older siblings. With the advent of a little brother or sister, the firstborn and other older children now find their positions seriously threatened. One way some experts have suggested to reduce the negative impact of new siblings is to pay careful attention to the spacing of your children's births.

SPACE SIBLINGS

Much of our understanding of the impact of siblings on self-confidence is incomplete and inconclusive. Still, the ongoing research is giving us a few ideas about how brothers and sisters interact with each other and some of the more interesting information and advice focuses on the issue of how to space your youngsters.

Some common advice you'll hear is, "space your children so that they'll have the time and room to be themselves and reach their potential." Usually, this means you should have them about three years apart, after each has a chance to develop pretty far past the toddler stage.

Psychiatrist Lee Salk, for example, recommends three-year spacing because earlier than that—say at age two and one half—children tend to be much more negatively oriented. Consequently, the arrival of a new sibling may cause more intense feelings of rivalry in the older siblings.

But recent research has called this traditional wisdom into question. In a survey of more than 1,700 American male teenagers, Dr. Jeannie Kidwell, a psychologist at the University of Tennessee, found that youngsters regarded themselves and their parents more negatively when only two years separated them from their siblings. On the other hand, when the siblings were less than a year or more than four years apart, the negative attitudes disappeared.

Apparently, children who are separated by only two years are most likely to compete more strenuously for their parents' attention throughout their lives. In contrast, those who are separated by only a year seem to sense that sharing their parents' attention with another child is quite natural because they've never experienced anything else. As a result, there's less resentment of the older child toward the younger one.

Along these same lines, research at Colorado State University has demonstrated that firstborn children who experience the birth of a young sibling when they're two years old have a lower self-esteem than those who are less than two years old when their siblings are born. But apparently, there is a kind of cut-off point for the negative impact produced by the younger sibling. In other words, about when a child reaches age five, he's able to maintain a relatively high level of self-esteem, despite the birth of another child in the family.

"A spacing of about five years is apparently optimal," Dr. Kidwell told a reporter from the *New York Times*. "It frees the parent from having to meet the demands and pressures of two children close together in age, thus allowing parents and children more time in one-to-one interaction for a more supportive and relaxed relationship."

Dr. Kidwell's research also suggests that similar principles apply for the spacing of births involving middle-born children. So, feelings of competition and lower self-esteem are characteristic of middle-born youngsters with siblings within two or three years. But when the spacing is greater than four years or less than two, the impact on self-esteem and relations between siblings is less.

Although this research is quite interesting and may be helpful in providing guidelines to parents who have considerable control over the spacing of their children, there are limits to how far we can take this basic issue. In fact, one of the leading researchers in this field, Dr. Robert Zajonc, a University of Michigan psychologist, says, "I would not advocate any pattern of spacing of children because many other factors are completely unknown."

As for me, I find the less-than-two-years or more-than-four-years arguments to be reasonably convincing—*if* you can fit this approach into your family planning. But perhaps you can't. I couldn't! After all, there are many valid reasons why couples *cannot* space their children a certain number of years apart. For example, the mother may want (or be forced) to get back into the working world as quickly as possible. Or birth control may fail. Or the older mother may face a limited number of childbearing years.

Even if you do manage to space your children at least three years apart, it's still quite likely that newcomers will bring significant new challenges to youthful self-confidence. And the first to feel the heat will be the older child or children.

THE DILEMMA OF THE DISPLACED OLDER CHILD

A second child will always have some significant impact on your firstborn. And if that first child is two years old or older, the impact will probably be all the more obvious.

For example, you can resign yourself to the likelihood that your two-year-old will revert to some infantile personality traits, like forgetting his toilet training. Why is this? The main problem for your two-year-old is that he'll sense a tremendous threat of *separation*.

Even if you're hospitalized for only a few days, being apart from you will bother him a great deal. Then, when you bring the new baby home, the separation will continue because now another human entity has come between you and your firstborn. Inevitably, both the physical and emotional intimacy between the two of you will decrease.

Children who are somewhat older, say ages three to five, will also have to wrestle with this threat of separation. But the older they get, the better the defenses they are able to employ.

For one thing, they will have learned how to turn to people other than the mother for support. Also, older children are able to wait for increasingly longer periods of time for gratification. So, if Mom isn't able to look after their needs right now, they'll be better equipped emotionally to wait for her for at least a few minutes. In short, the older preschoolers are becoming more independent of the mother. Consequently, the threat to their position in the family and to their basic identity is not so great when the new child arrives.

But two-year-olds are a different proposition!

The problem with these younger firstborns can become so severe that doctors and nurses these days routinely warn new mothers of second children about it. Also, many hospitals are starting programs to acquaint older siblings with hospital procedures and to get them involved with the birth of the baby. That way, the firstborns tend to feel they have more of a vested interest in the newcomer and are more likely to accept the younger child with greater equanimity. A kind of "sibling bonding" takes place.

A major problem that plagues many mothers with the arrival of a second child—and makes the firstborn feel neglected—is the tremendous fatigue that grips the woman who finds herself the primary caretaker for two small children.

The baby books that you read will tell you the basics of this problem: They'll say you're going to be exhausted . . . you'll have physical aches and pains . . . you should have someone coming to your home for the first two months or so to help with the cooking and cleaning.

If you decide to nurse your new youngster, there will be an added energy drain. Also, there's almost always a tendency for the mother to focus most of her attention on the new child. At the same time, she may let other matters in the family slide, including her relationship with her firstborn.

The resulting upheaval in the older child's physical and emotional relationship with his mother can be devastating. And he has a ready object to blame for all his troubles—his newborn sibling.

The scene is now set for the first explosions in an ongoing round of sibling salvos! It certainly isn't difficult to understand how an older child—especially one who is only a couple of years older than the younger—can develop deep and sometimes long-lasting hostility toward the younger sibling.

But destructive sibling rivalry and hatred aren't inevitable. In fact, this reaction can be softened, if not mostly eliminated, if parents are aware of what's coming. And the more you can do to limit a hostile reaction on the part of the firstborn, the more you'll contribute to the growth of solid self-confidence in both your children.

What practical steps can you take to head off these sibling salvos?

A second-line caretaker, often the father, may be able to devote extra time and attention to the firstborn, who is feeling somewhat left out by all the attention being showered on the new child. Of course, it's not realistic to expect Dad to step in suddenly as a total mother substitute, especially if he hasn't already played a significant role in the older child's life. The same limitations apply to a grandmother or other temporary mother substitute.

Consequently, it's important for the father, grandmother or some other family member to lay the groundwork for a close relationship with the firstborn *before* the second child arrives. In other words, the father might begin to play with the older youngster more often; read more; and otherwise spend more time with his two-year-old before the new sibling comes onto the scene. That way, the older child will become accustomed to the father's increased presence and in-volvement, and the transition to having two children in the family should be much smoother.

In addition, the parents shouldn't become too overbearing or con-trolling in trying to orchestrate the relationship between the two siblings. It's important for both father and mother to *respect* the evolving relationship between the older and younger child. That's the only way that either will develop an independent sense of their respective identities—and lay solid foundations for self-confidence.

Phoebe Prosky, a family therapist with the Ackerman Institute for

Family Therapy in New York, puts it this way: "They [the parents] must develop a wisdom, a sense of when to step in and help form that relationship, and when to step back and let it seek its own level."

One way to keep perspective on sibling rivalry is to see the humor in it. At the age of two and a half, little Emily, who at the time was the only child in her family, made it clear that she resented being called a baby.

"No, I'm big girl!" she would insist when someone even implied that she was barely out of infancy.

But then, her parents had another child, and the whole situation changed. Emily would watch jealously as her mother held the newcomer during a large part of each day and gave the baby almost all her attention.

"You're getting to be such a big girl!" one of her neighbors said on one occasion.

But Emily replied, "No, I'm a baby too!"

Fortunately, by the time her little sister was about six months old, Emily began to outgrow her resentment of the intruder. But as with many other siblings, Emily's sense of rivalry and competition still lingered on in some form. Although the parents laughed about Emily's change of heart, they knew they had to devote more time and attention to her so that she wouldn't feel left out. They wanted to blunt the hostility she felt toward her little sister. So the parents arranged their personal schedules so that they could each spend more time alone with Emily during this transition period, when the newcomer was being integrated into the family.

Though parents can devote more time to individual youngsters and encourage peaceful play relationships, they can't control all the details of the interactions between the older and younger child. In many ways they can only provide a constructive environment for sibling relationships. To encourage this, Mom and Dad need to retain their ability to laugh and joke when friction develops between two siblings. Even in the midst of conflict, they also need to encourage and support each child in his or her respective course of development.

In short, self-confidence can be encouraged, but it can't be *imposed* from the outside. The best that you as a parent can often do is to act as a facilitator and guide to healthy sibling relationships and perhaps step in when conflicts begin to get out of hand. Your children have to learn to grapple with their own problems and solve them as much as possible by themselves. Parents who tinker too much with a youngster's ability to try to stand up for himself may engender excessive dependence rather than independent self-assurance.

On the other hand, things do sometimes get totally out of order between siblings. At those times parents can help correct excessive and perhaps even dangerous tendencies in a child. One such tendency to look for is the emergence of bully traits in your youngster.

THE BIRTH OF A BULLY

What causes a child to become a bully?

There are many reasons. One common thread that seems to run through many such personalities is the need to compensate for a deep sense of inadequacy or lack of acceptance by one in authority. In other cases, bullying traits may emerge because youngsters lack good parental models or because they fail to identify with socially adept parents. In one 22-year study conducted by psychologists Leonard Evan and L. Rowell Huesmann of the University of Chicago, children with bullying traits were shown to develop such traits by age six. Furthermore, they continued to be overly aggressive, unpopular and even criminally oriented into adulthood. What can parents of such children do? When the children are quite young, the researchers say, the parents should project themselves as good social role models and encourage their youngsters to identify more with them.

Sometimes, the obnoxious trait will emerge out of deep feelings of jealousy or rage that occur when a younger sibling comes on the scene. The older can't bear it when the younger seems to be supplanting the older child's position with the parents. If the parents fail to step in and give the older youngster a feeling of acceptance and importance, the results may be disastrous.

One little four-year-old girl, Mary, was apprehensive when she learned that her mother was going to give birth. Unfortunately, her parents did nothing to make her feel more comfortable. So her anxiety about the situation increased as the day of the birth approached.

After her baby brother was born, her worst fears were realized: Her mother devoted what seemed to the girl to be overwhelming amounts of time to the baby. Moreover, the father had eyes only for his new son, who had been given his name. And all the relatives and friends of the family focused their attention on the little boy.

Understandably, the older daughter was upset at this turn of events. Suddenly, she seemed to have been "dethroned" and cast in the role of outsider. Because no one explained to her that she was still loved and respected, her attitude got worse. Furthermore, the growing hostility she felt began to focus solely on the most obvious target—her younger sibling.

Within two to three years, this daughter's behavior toward her brother had become almost vicious. Also, she began loudly and repeatedly voicing her dislike for boys in general, calling them worthless and "nothing but trouble." Playing the part of a strict disciplinarian, Mary even went so far as to give the younger child orders that she knew he would not obey. Then, his "disobedience" would provide her with an opportunity to administer her own brand of punishment—usually barring him from playing with the other children and perhaps sending him home.

She even resorted to meting out physical punishment, such as pushing the little boy, throwing him to the ground and pulling his hair. A neighbor I interviewed couldn't remember ever seeing these two siblings play successfully together.

Obviously, Mary's feelings of hostility were major league—truly destructive, and maybe even dangerous. But what could be done in such a situation?

The first thing was for the parents to recognize how serious the problem was. But even after that breakthrough, there was still a great amount of work to be done.

One problem that emerged during counseling sessions was that the mother, wanting to pursue certain part-time career interests, had chosen to spend very little time with Mary. She had concentrated on the younger child, the victimized boy, for a couple of years. But then, she turned both of them over to a series of baby-sitters. As a result, they both lacked close supervision, and Mary had filled in the gap with her own brand of tough, destructive discipline over her brother.

Clearly, Mary was a tragic example of a child who lacked self-confidence. And, as too often happens, she wasn't receiving any parental support to help her develop it. She had no good parental role model for proper social behavior. Also, she wasn't around either parent enough to give her an opportunity to identify with their good qualities. So she made sense of her world in the only way she knew how: She kept her threatening younger brother under her heel by imposing a series of inflexible, and often unfair, childish rules on him.

Predictably, Mary's conduct also had a damaging effect on her brother. As the passive partner in their relationship, he found his own self-confidence impeded by her constant bullying. Certainly, he had started out as the center of attention. But after he passed through the toddler stage, he was no longer the only cute little baby on the block; so the adults began to shift their interest elsewhere.

These parents and children are still trying to work out their problems. The mother has at least become aware that she is a large part of the problem, and she's trying to make some adjustments in her life-style. But it's difficult for her. She's having to reorient her entire value system so that her priorities center more on her children than on herself.

The father also has to make some changes in his life. Although he started out overtly favoring the son over the daughter, his relationship with both children became much more distant as time went on. His work schedule and outside interests—particularly a demanding tennis schedule that he had set up for himself—filled up time that he might otherwise have spent with his family. So he has had to try to change his approach to life, though he hasn't been entirely successful.

In this case, time and attention from the parents are the only factors that seem to have a chance of turning the situation around. This little bully and her sibling victim need more guidance and direction from on high. That's the only way that either of them can hope to recover a solid sense of identity and get back on the road to self-confidence.

TRIPLE PLAYS

The sibling salvos usually begin during the preschool years, just after the second child is born. But the conflict may increase in intensity all through childhood and the teen years. In fact, the wounds may never fully heal, even after all the brothers and sisters have reached adulthood.

In most cases, the most intense conflicts seem to occur if the younger child is born before the older one has reached school age. Children in the early school age group—say, from ages six to ten—often react to the birth of a younger sibling with indifference. There may be some excitement when the new child is born. But the older child is usually deeply involved with his peer relationships and the challenge of learning new skills at school and on the athletic field. So he has very little time for siblings, especially those who are six years or more his junior.

But if the younger sibling comes along while the older is still a toddler or a preschooler, there's more fertile ground for serious problems and conflicts. In this case, as the two get older, the dynamics between them can become extremely intricate—indeed, almost Byzantine. The problems may multiply considerably if a third sibling is born during the period when the first two are trying to work out their own conflicts and positions in the family.

I call a complex three-way relationship between siblings, at least two of whom are close in age, a "triple play." For example, in one family where there was an older brother, a boy one year his junior and a sister who was five years younger than the middle child, the two boys waged an intense competition with one another practically from the cradle. Many times, their sister became a pawn in the struggle.

At first the sister was the younger brother's ally. But then she began to resent the competition that constantly broke out between them because they were both athletically inclined. After this competition began to heat up between the two younger siblings, the older boy became the natural ally of the youngest, the little girl. Now, the *middle* brother was the one who was consistently excluded from the "inner circle" of sibling relationships in the family.

Rather complicated, wouldn't you say? Still, such sibling dynamics are commonplace in most families. And if the parents are not sensitive to what's going on, and to the *changing* dynamics, one child or more may be badly bruised.

In this case, the middle child, the younger brother, is the one who suffered most. The eldest, the older boy, grew up to become a high achiever, both in school and the professional world. The youngest, the girl, wasn't as achievement oriented but she had a firm sense of who she was and what she needed to do to be reasonably satisfied in life. As a result, she found steady employment, married happily and settled down to become a solid, satisfied member of her community.

The middle child, on the other hand, spent years casting about, trying to determine who he was and how he fit into the world. His main problem was that he had become profoundly uncertain about his abilities.

He never was as good in his studies as his older brother, so he fell short by that comparison. On the other hand, he was not as gregarious, likable or athletic as his younger sister. Because he couldn't measure up—at least in his own eyes—to his two siblings in these ways, he tended to feel inferior for a long time.

Finally, when he reached his early thirties, he settled on a career in business—an entrepreneurial venture that satisfied his need to be independent and be himself. Because he was reasonably successful, he finally began to derive some sense of satisfaction in life. But still he harbored feelings of rivalry with his siblings—and a sense of inadequacy because he felt he had never really managed to equal them.

Of course, this all might have turned out differently if the children had formed different sibling alliances. For instance, if the two brothers had formed a common front against the sister instead of competing for her support, the younger boy would probably have emerged much more sure of himself. But the girl in this case might have found that her self-confidence was being severely undermined.

Obviously, we can't be certain how the situation might have turned out differently. But one thing is sure: The parents should have been more attentive to the need to strengthen the self-confidence of *each* of these children. In that case, all the siblings would almost surely have turned out much better.

One moral of this little story is that it's absolutely essential for parents to be very sensitive to the emotional needs of each of their children at various ages. Also, parents must be aware that their youngsters may very well conflict with one another head-on. At times, most certainly, the siblings will support each other, but at other times, there's no doubt that they'll have problems with one another.

You can help all your youngsters to understand these interactions by talking and working with them. It won't do just to get angry that they're fighting and send them to their rooms as punishment. As a last resort, such discipline may be necessary. But before you ever reach that point, it's important to explore the deeper dimensions of their three-way relationship. Then, analyze what impact each is having on the self-confidence of the others, and respond accordingly.

In any case, there's no fixed formula for handling a "triple play" relationship—especially in so far as that relationship may bear upon a child's self-confidence. For instance, a result completely different from that of the first example was reached with three other children: the firstborn, Kathi, the second-born, Patti, and the "baby" of the family, Henry.

Kathi, a plump, happy and contented youngster, was not quite two years old when Patti was born. From that moment, Kathi developed an intense jealousy of this interloper—so much so, that the parents were advised not to leave the two sisters alone together for fear that Kathi would behave violently toward Patti.

The younger girl, Patti, grew much as many child-rearing experts would have predicted: She clamored for attention and affection, and in general became a little spitfire.

Meanwhile, Kathi, after getting over her early hostility, became a rather quiet, composed, ladylike little figure. She even developed a considerable degree of inner confidence after she had been assured by her parents, and particularly her mother, that she still had a special place in the family as the firstborn.

In addition to her parental support, Kathi was able to increase her self-confidence because she consistently outdid Patti in her schoolwork. Patti, for her part, resented Kathi's superior performance. Before long, she developed a kind of inferiority complex because of her sister's superior braininess.

To compensate, Patti turned to sports—with considerable success. Both girls took tennis lessons and became quite good players, but Patti was the real "killer" on the court. She attacked the game with an aggressiveness that eventually made her a tournament player before she was 10 years old. Kathi was a graceful, stylish player but she lacked Patti's competitive fire.

In later years, Kathi married and became a contented mother and outstanding volunteer worker in community activities. But Patti could never go that route. Her early aggressiveness—the only apparent means she had of asserting her own importance and sense of identity—carried over when she finally entered the business world. She became a highly paid executive and for all appearances was a "success," perhaps even more so than her older sister.

But in a revealing comment stated in the course of an interview, she referred to herself, without attempting to be funny, as "daughter number two" in the family. In other words, she still felt she was playing second fiddle to her older sister.

There was also a third child in this family—a boy by the name of Henry. It's easy to forget him because he came along ten years after Kathi and eight years after Patti. In some ways he was like an only child because he had been born so many years after his two siblings. But actually his situation was different from that of an only child because he had two older sisters who, even though they fought between themselves, doted on him.

So Henry grew up supported by a loving father who was overjoyed to have a son, and four devoted females—his grandmother, his mother and his two sisters. Kathi became his surrogate mother when he was in trouble; Patti was his role model in athletics.

Henry was a picture of success and self-confidence. He became an outstanding sportsman and scholar and went on to get a doctorate in marine science. His great self-assurance, which was evident to all, derived from the fact that he suffered *no* sibling putdowns; rather, he was showered with love by all family members. This may all sound a bit syrupy, but after all, love is—or should be—the most potent force for good in family life. And it's certainly important to youthful self-confidence.

Of course, not all of us enjoy such a supportive environment when we're growing up. But an atmosphere similar to that which nurtured Henry is what every parent should strive to provide for his or her children. The closer the youngsters are in age, the more difficult the task will be. But that's where it is crucial for the parents to focus appropriate time and attention on those sons and daughters who need it the most.

Perhaps it's inevitable that when there are several children in the family, one or more will feel less competent than the others. But I'm not willing to be quite this fatalistic.

Time and attention by the parents are two key ingredients that can help foster self-confidence in a child. But you have to *make* time for your youngster and *give* her attention. For most of us, providing the right kind of time and attention requires a plan or strategy. In other words, as we mentioned in an earlier chapter, you need to develop a "self-confidence plan" that will serve as a guideline to build your child's self-confidence. A key part of this plan must be to explore the special gifts and talents of *each* child. Attempting to treat all children the same will inevitably be inappropriate for some. Because this approach takes thought, care and understanding, speak to teachers and other experts for guidance.

In practically every case in which one or more children reach adulthood without sufficient self-confidence, there seems to have been a lack of time and attention given them by their parents. Does this sound like I'm trying to encourage guilt feelings in you? Then so be it! As parents, you have serious, weighty responsibilities. The more children you have, the more serious those responsibilities are.

So when you find yourself in one of these "triple play" situations, with three or more children in your charge, take time to investigate exactly what's going on among them. See how each is affecting the other. Then resign yourself to the fact that you're going to have to double your child-rearing time with two children, and *triple* that time with three. In fact, two will probably take three times as much time and effort, and three will probably take four times as much time and effort!

If you fail to plan your strategy, to set aside sufficient time and to make sufficient effort, you can expect to see at least one and perhaps more of your children grow up without a full measure of self-confidence. And that will mean this son or daughter won't reach his or her full potential.

But *with* an effective strategy by parents, children can expect to increase their self-confidence and self-esteem. One important factor in such a strategy must be an understanding of the implications of a youngster's place in the sibling birth order.

THE BEST, THE BRIGHTEST, AND BIRTH ORDER

Whenever a family includes more than one child, the issue of the impact of birth order almost always arises. Fatalistic as it may sound, the order of your children's birth plays a major—and sometimes decisive—role in determining the degree of success they achieve.

But you can't always predict which child will have the most self-confidence. At this point, by the way, it's important to distinguish once more between self-confidence and high achievement. Those children who achieve the most are not necessarily the most self-confident. Conversely, the most self-confident don't necessarily hit the top among their siblings in achievement.

Remember, we've defined self-confidence in a rather broad way: A person who is self-confident is one who is not only in a position to realize his potential for outward success; he's also able to weather the ups and downs of life. In general, he has the capacity to be content and satisfied. In short, a self-confident person is one who is secure with his particular position in life and not constantly looking to others to define his goals and directions.

You may find that the oldest child in the family has achieved the most. But the middle youngster or the youngest may be the most secure and well-adjusted. Still, a child's position in the family can affect both his potential for self-confidence and his later success. So what can you, as a parent, do to affect positively the impact of birth order?

First of all, it's necessary to have an understanding of what the likely effects of sibling position will be on a child. Here's a little quiz to test your knowledge of the subject. Are the following statements true or false?

S: Except for the mentally handicapped, all siblings in a given family tend to possess approximately the same I.Q.'s.
A: *False*. Typically, the oldest child enjoys the highest I.Q. The next sibling rates somewhat lower and so on down the line.

Research by Dr. Robert Zajonc, a psychologist at the University of Michigan, has revealed that a number of family factors, including birth order, will influence a child's intelligence and performance on standardized tests. In general, for example, children in smaller families do better on intelligence tests than children in larger families. Also, siblings who are spaced further apart tend to score higher.

Why is this? No one knows for sure, but there are several theories. For one thing, the first child's environment is clearly different from that of the succeeding children. So, the first child tends to get all the available adult attention, while younger children have to share it.

Also, the oldest child has the opportunity to act as "teacher" to younger siblings; this role can help to sharpen his mental skills.

> S: First children are apt to be the more successful siblings because they have the greatest self-confidence.
>
> A: *True* and *False*. This statement is true in that the superachievers in this world are often eldest children. According to some experts on children, the firstborns of this world are known as the "officer class" because they tend to dominate their younger siblings and have the strongest aspirations to take the lead in the grown-up world.

A psychologist who has written a book on the implications of birth order, Kevin Leman, says "If you look at achievers, it correlates with birth order." As an example, he notes that of the first 23 astronauts, 21 were the oldest children in their families. (*Wall Street Journal*, August 21, 1986)

These findings are confirmed by studies in other fields. A political scientist at the University of Louisville, Paul J. Weber, has reported that a relatively large number of U.S. Supreme Court justices have been eldest children.

On the other hand, among siblings in a family firstborns are not necessarily the most self-confident. As we've seen, true self-confidence has many facets. Firstborns may tend to be the greater achievers, but that may arise from the fact that they feel *in*secure in some ways and are trying to compensate for this by outward accomplishments.

> S: One reason for the high achievement of firstborn children is that parents tend to have higher expectations for them than for the other youngsters in the family.
>
> A: *True*. Dr. Walter Toman, a former psychology professor at Brandeis University, conducted studies of nearly 3,000 people over a period of 30 years as to the impact of birth order. He found that firstborns tend to have a much stronger achievement orientation than their other siblings—and he argues that the reason for this is higher parental expectations for the oldest child.

Parents tend to harbor images of their firstborn as president of the United States, a major success in the business world, or a great leader in the arts. Many times, these ambitions for the first child are projections of achievements that Mom and Dad wish they could have attained. As a result, the child is much more likely to be named after a parent or some other esteemed family member.

Depending on how these parental aspirations are expressed, the child may develop more self-confidence—*or* less. In other words, if a parent puts great pressure on a firstborn to live up to adult expectations, the child may turn into a frustrated perfectionist. Or he may otherwise experience extreme self-doubts when he fails to live up to parental preconceptions. Placing such pressure on a firstborn certainly won't enhance his development of self-confidence.

On the other hand, if parents approach their expectations and aspirations for their first child with a degree of flexibility, warmth and love, the child may interpret those adult expectations as signs of confidence that the parents have in him. If the youngster senses that his parents think he can do something—and he doesn't feel that there will be dire consequences or great disappointment if he doesn't—he'll be more likely to develop a sense of assurance.

S: The youngest children are the most deprived in enjoying a family atmosphere that breeds self-confidence.

A: *False*. A younger child *may* lack self-confidence. On the other hand, he may have a great deal of self-confidence.

One of the factors that works in favor of self-confidence in younger children is that they are less dependent on external support than the older child, and especially support from their parents. Consequently, they'll usually experience less pressure from their parents to live up to adult expectations, especially to fulfill Mommy's or Daddy's unsatisfied needs or dreams.

Some enlightened parents are becoming more sensitive to the special position of younger children. Because younger siblings *do* have some disadvantages, such as a tendency to develop a lower I.Q. or to be lower achievers, some parents are spending more time with them. They're helping these youngsters develop in areas that otherwise might have been neglected.

In this regard, it's important for parents to read to their younger children as much as they did to the older one. Also, mothers and fathers should try to spend as much time with them in their younger, developmental years as they did with the firstborn. To even approach this goal will take organization of time and effort, especially since many mothers plan to return to work earlier with the second child because of increased financial obligations. '

S: Middle-born children—that is, those who are not the oldest or the youngest—tend to be overlooked by parents, develop insecure personalities and are more likely to rebel against parental authority.

A: *True* and *false*. It's true, according to Dr. Jeannie Kidwell, a psychologist at the University of Tennessee, that middle-born children often have lower self-esteem than do their older or younger siblings. On the other hand, as we've already indicated, if the spacing between these middle-born youngsters and their other siblings is four years or more, their view of themselves, including their self-confidence, tends to be higher.

Also, the sex of the older sibling is quite important in influencing the level of self-esteem of the middle-born. If the older sibling is the *same* sex as the middle-born child, the middle-born tends to have lower self-esteem. On the other hand, if the oldest child is of the opposite sex, the middle-born youngster is more likely to have greater self-esteem and self-confidence. Dr. Kidwell believes that having an older sibling of the opposite sex gives the middle-born youngster a sense of being special, and that works to raise the self-esteem of the middle-born.

Some researchers have argued that middle-children tend to be relatively good negotiators and peacemakers because they've had to develop flexibility and the capacity to compromise in order to survive successfully between their older and younger siblings. Sometimes, though, they may have a sense of being "kicked around," persecuted or ignored by parents and peers. As one *Wall Street Journal* writer observed, "Richard Nixon may be the classic middle-child." (*Wall Street Journal*, August 21, 1986)

Unfortunately, the strengths of the middle-child may be diminishing in our society, because according to the latest figures reported by the U.S. Census Bureau, the numbers of middle children are declining. In 1970, 36 percent of American families with children had at least three youngsters, but by 1985, that percentage had dropped to 20 percent. A number of experts feel that this decline in three-child families is likely to continue.

S: At best, only children tend to be loners, outsiders and generally unsociable. At worst, they're self-centered, spoiled brats.

A: *False*. In fact, according to Dr. Toni Falbo, a University of Texas psychologist, only children tend to have a number of distinct advantages. After reviewing more than 200 studies in her recent report, *The Single Child Family*, Dr. Falbo concluded that only children have the following:

- more of a sense of independence and emotional maturity by the time they enter college;
- higher intelligence during childhood than children with one or more siblings; and
- higher incomes and greater career prestige as adults.

Eric L. Lang, a researcher at the University of Michigan, speculates that the high mental acuity of the only child may result from exposure "primarily to his or her parents' well-developed vocabularies and adult decision processes. This type of environment facilitates the child's mental growth." (*New York Times*, February 16, 1986, letter to the editor)

In addition, Judith Blake, a demographer at UCLA who has studied the impact of family size on children, says that only children may be more outgoing and have more friends than youngsters with siblings.

Many high-achieving only children in our society tend to support this positive view of youngsters without siblings. A few successful only children in our culture include takeover specialists Carl Icahn and T. Boone Pickens, actor Cary Grant, journalist Ted Koppel, model/actress Brooke Shields, pro quarterback Joe Montana and author John Updike. With the recent decrease in family size in the United States, the number of families with only children has been on the rise. An estimated 22 percent of families with children now have only one child, up from 13 percent in 1964.

Obviously, this question of the impact of birth order is a complex one. Higher intelligence and achievement *may* help to enhance a child's self-confidence. On the other hand, these qualities, if they are combined with unreasonable, inappropriate or high-pressured expectations from parents, may develop without sufficient self-confidence.

It's impossible to be exactly the same with each child. As the years pass, you become a different person and, consequently, you relate to each of your children in a different way. Also, the dynamics of having more than one child in the family inevitably will affect the way that each of your children develops. But if you make an effort to be evenhanded with each of your children, that will go a long way toward giving all of them some of the advantages of being a firstborn.

Also, it's important for parents to be as relaxed as possible in guiding the firstborn through each of the developmental phases. If you apply too much pressure or are too rigid in pressing your preconceived notions, your efforts are likely to backfire. So even as you treat your later-born children as firstborns, you should also treat your firstborn as a later-born!

Again, I know you can't achieve the impossible. Certainly, in many ways your firstborn will *be* a firstborn; your youngest will behave as the youngest; and your middle-born will probably possess some of the traits of others born at a similar place in the birth order. There are definite limits on the degree to which you can change any of this. On the other hand, if you give your children a relatively free reign to develop, you'll probably find that they are in a better position to become not only relatively high achievers, but also self-confident achievers. And what parent could ask for more than that?

7

Crisis Four: Peer Competition

The Scene: A sandbox in a playground in Anytown, U.S.A.

The characters: A group of two-year-olds, and another group of three- and four-year-olds.

The action: The two groups are playing separately. There's a distinct difference in the way each group plays. Each of the two-year-olds, largely lost in his or her own tiny world, is playing alone. One or more may be copying another's type of play, but there's no interaction between children. In the jargon of the experts, this is known as "parallel play."

But things are different with the older children: They're obviously interacting. Some push a toy dump truck back and forth among themselves. Others work together, building little turrets for a sandcastle.

Now, we're getting to a growth phase that sets the tone of a child's self-confidence for years to come. All that has come before in a child's life has been pointing toward this event—the intense interactions between children which usually indicate how they will compete and cooperate later in life.

The older children in the above scene are involved in what is known as "collaborative play," which involves cooperation to produce a result that the children could not accomplish alone. They have found that they can enjoy working together on a common project—an insight that goes to the very heart of the development of true self-confidence.

By my definition, self-confident people function easily and smoothly as part of a team. They take pride in their performance as a group, as well as in their achievements as individuals. These individuals are not loners, not inner-directed geniuses or obsessive artists, however brilliant, who suffer tunnel vision in social situations.

In short, true self-confidence involves not only what you can do *by* yourself, but also what you can do *with* others. Can you lead them effectively? Do you know how to be a good follower?

Success and happiness in adulthood usually depend heavily on a sense of assurance in employing these cooperative skills. They depend on a "team temperament," which is an ability to cooperate with others even as you do your best as an individual. A team temperament incorporates a healthy attitude toward competition, including an ability to be both a good winner and a good loser. There's simply no room for the "killer" competitor in most of the upper echelons of our society. Nor is there room for the person who is incapable of working effectively with others. If your youngster tends to be a "loner" or encounters great difficulty in sharing and playing with his peers, he may be in danger of not developing this team temperament, which is an important ingredient of self-confidence.

Around age three, you will probably see—and definitely should encourage—cooperation that goes beyond sandbox projects. At this stage, children can recognize that their peers are independent entities with their own different feelings and thoughts. At the same time, your child will gravitate toward children who complement his own interests. He'll begin to take pleasure in the fact that there are things he can share, even if that sharing involves physical roughhousing and "cutting up."

As silly and childish as this play may seem to parents, mothers and fathers should definitely encourage these developments by providing an environment and equipment that will foster it. The other day, while watching a group of three-year-olds at our neighborhood playground, I noticed that they preferred games that included two or more players. They liked the swings, where one could ride and another push. They also liked to try out the child-propelled merry-go-round equipment that operates on the same principle. It's not that they were particularly adept at these activities. The important thing was that they were beginning to play together. They were moving slowly past the two-year-old plea, "Mommy, push me."

Of course, this dependence on parents won't pass completely for years. Your youngster may still want to be carried, pushed or otherwise helped by adults, even after he reaches school age. Still, when he reaches three, the promise of peer collaboration will become more and more tantalizing, and should grow steadily through adulthood.

But as I say, the first steps toward peer interaction are halting at best. It's only later, at the age of five to six, that children begin to incorporate more elaborate rules that they may make up—or borrow from what they've heard from adults—to govern their games and their fantasies. Now, the teamwork begins to get more complex: You make rules for others to follow, and you follow their rules as well.

TEAMWORK

Why is the development of a teamwork temperament so important?

More and more in business, teamwork is required of all employees, even top executives. No longer does just one person make all the major decisions. Instead, there may be a fairly broad base of major decision makers in a given company. In fact, some large corporations such as J.C. Penney have established an "office of the chairman," which includes several top-ranking executives invested with major decision-making powers. At the lower management levels, there has been an increased emphasis on consensus decision making, where teams of middle- and upper-middle management executives put their heads together and settle major issues jointly.

Even that seemingly individualistic profession, medicine, has begun to surrender to the teamwork concept. I know this from long personal experience.

Often, the successful medical student will charge through his education, operating as a keen competitor and getting excellent grades. But when he begins his actual hospital work as an intern or resident, he discovers that individual excellence is not the only thing: Being a team player may be even more important.

Many times, I've found myself in the uncomfortable position of having to teach hotshot young doctors a fact of modern medical life:

Their decision making will be ineffectual unless they can function as part of a team of other doctors, nurses, clerical staff and family members. The team, and not the individual physician, however brilliant, is what treats and cures patients. Sometimes, we've even had to recommend that the "lone rangers" in medical practice should transfer from primary patient care and devote themselves to laboratory work or some other specialty that does not demand teamwork.

Some people just can't adjust to teamwork. But in most cases, early training, beginning around age three, will help nurture this all-important attribute in your child. Most preschools and elementary schools now recognize how important these socialization skills are. Instead of focusing only on what the individual child can produce, the teachers also look at how well she works with others and how well she plays in a group of his peers. This emphasis in schools is extremely healthy, and should serve as something of a model for the way parents train their children at home.

With the proper early training, a child should mature into a self-confident adult who can walk into a roomful of people, knowing that somehow, if he wants to, he can make himself fit in. The ultimate goal: He should learn to accommodate his interests to the interests of others, and he should know when to assert himself in a social situation and when to back off. Your success in helping your child develop this all-important team temperament demands keen observation, patient understanding, and great sensitivity to the youngster's changing needs and emotions.

As a corollary to all this, you might look at your own relationships with other adults. How well do you get along with them? How sensitive are you to the needs and reactions of others? If you fail to interact comfortably or effectively with *your* peers, in all probability you'll fail to one degree or another with your children. You simply won't have the knowledge to communicate to them how they should perform in group situations. So it may very well be that you'll need to start the process of developing a team temperament with yourself!

Even if you're not quite perfect in the way you relate to other adults, there's still plenty that you can do for your children. Let's consider some typical situations that occur in every family and examine how we should handle them to encourage teamwork rather than isolation or cutthroat competition.

Situation #1:   Johnny comes home from school, and you ask, "Let me see how your homework was graded. What did you get on that test today?"

Omission: You didn't also ask, "Whom were you playing with? Who's your best friend now? Did you play in any games with the other boys?"

Situation #2:   Johnny is playing with some of his friends, and he tries to pull their toys away from them. You react sharply: "Stop that, Johnny! Don't be so selfish!"

Omission: You didn't add, "Try to ask nicely for their toys. Say to them, 'May I use your scooter? You can play with my ball.'"

Situation #3:   Johnny is playing with his friends as in situation #2, and once again he tries to pull their toys away. You don't react at all. You just think, "Good, he's asserting himself. I want a dominant child."

Omission: You failed to see that Johnny is not interacting. Instead, he's interfering with cooperative play. It would have been better for you to step in and tell him that his treatment of his peers should involve more cooperation. Then, you can show him exactly how he should collaborate.

Situation #4:   Johnny has one favorite companion with whom he plays every day. They get along excellently, and you encourage the continuing relationship.

Omission: You haven't provided opportunities for Johnny to mingle with a number of children. As a result, he may turn into a "one-friend" child, and may tend to become intimidated in large groups.

Situation #5:   Jane has just started school, and you're naturally concerned about whether she was good or whether she acted up. Also, you want to know if she adjusted to her new surroundings easily. So you question her teacher about these issues.

Omission: You didn't ask the teacher how Jane behaved in a group and how she reacted to the other children. Perhaps the teacher didn't even pay any particular attention to Jane. But if you ask her a few key questions early in the school year, you can bet that she'll begin watching your youngster more closely and evaluating her progress.

Of course, you can't just follow a few practical suggestions like those mentioned above once and then drop the matter. Rather, you have to *reiterate* these and other points over and over again to your child so that the basic message isn't lost.

For example, if your youngster tends to be excessively "grabby" you might have to repeat a litany like this on a fairly regular basis until the point sinks in: "Jack is coming over to play with you today because he likes you and he enjoys playing with your toys. But if you take the toys away from him all the time, he may not want to come here anymore."

At first, you may think you're just talking to yourself—especially when your child reacts negatively to what you're saying. But if you keep at it in a nice, low-key, reasonably positive fashion, the principles of cooperative play will begin to sink in. And you'll be well on your way to establishing the beginnings of a teamwork temperament that is so important to later self-confidence.

Also, a similar principle applies to schoolteachers or other adults who are in charge of your youngster for part of the day. You'll want to raise the same questions on a regular basis about your child's inter-actions with his peers. You don't want to become a pest. But you do want to make it clear that your interest in your child—and your desire to monitor and shape her behavior—is ongoing.

Some very exciting and complex things begin to happen to children at about age four to five, both as individuals and as members of a peer group. You start seeing an explosion of concrete skills, and more subtly, you notice their dawning realization that they can accomplish more with their friends than they can alone. At the same time, these preschoolers begin to identify themselves as unique and different individuals. Also, paradoxically, they begin to reach out for exciting role models to follow.

At this stage, it's normal—and by no means a sign of a lack of self-confidence—for a child to develop a series of crushes on older children, clergy or scout leaders. Also, there's a tendency to "go along with the crowd," rather than assert independence and in-dividuality among peers. Your child is now walking a fine line between budding individualism on the one hand and peer pressure and conformity on the other. In the midst of this high-wire act, he's constantly trying to achieve his balance by relying on role models provided by parents and other adults.

It's a difficult performance for a youngster, no doubt about that! If your youngster buckles under to much peer pressure, he'll fail to develop his unique capacities as an individual. On the other hand, if he operates too much as an individual, focusing almost exclusively on his private skills and interests, he won't develop the cooperative skills necessary for self-confidence and success in later life.

I'm reminded of the dilemma faced by one family whose five-year-old son was quite gregarious and also possessed an above-average intellectual aptitude. But they worried that he would fail to utilize his intellectual capacity because he always seemed to want to please his peers more than he wanted to concentrate on his kindergarten assignments.

Admittedly, these parents may have been worrying too much about minor matters. The child was doing quite well in his development on the whole, and there would be plenty of time in the next few years for them to instruct him in how to work hard, concentrate on his studies, and achieve his full potential academically.

On the other hand, I'm a great believer in watching for early signals in childhood development and responding to them as soon as possible. In this way, you can often head off big problems before they have a chance to develop.

In this case, the parents wisely avoided getting overly concerned about their youngster's early tendencies. At the same time, they began to emphasize that he had to "be his own person" and not allow himself to be distracted by his peers when they weren't following the teacher's directions. In effect, these parents just shifted the rudder in their child's development a little this way and that, from month to month, as they watched his early development. They gently encouraged the strengths they saw in him and helped him as soon as possible to compensate for apparent weaknesses.

In many ways, using a boat as a metaphor is apt here. If you're navigating a boat, and you allow it to drift off course, it will take much longer to reach your destination. In fact, under such circumstances, you may *never* reach it. So it's important to make course corrections at points along the way if you hope to make port.

It's much the same with a child. The parent who is always watchful and concerned will be in a much better position to step in before a child's life gets too far off course and the opportunities to set matters straight have been lost. But the course corrections must be made with warm and loving attention to a child's development, not with the heavy hand often used by pushy, highly competitive parents.

THE PERILS OF PUSHY PARENTHOOD

In their laudable concern to rear well-rounded, self-confident, success-oriented children, many parents go to ridiculous extremes. They've been comparing their youngster with his peers from an early age, and they're determined to do everything they can to give him advantages in the ongoing competitions of life. Such parental feelings usually intensify during the preschool years, when peer relations become so important.

Most upwardly mobile mothers and fathers want to give their children the greatest advantages possible in life. But it's important to distinguish between *providing* children with advantages in education, culture and physical development, and *overburdening* them with self-defeating cram courses in these same subjects.

Pundit Marie Winn has observed,

> The Age of Protection has ended. The Age of Preparation has set in. And children have suffered a loss. As they are integrated at a young age into the adult world, their lives have become more difficult, more confusing—in short, more like adult lives.

Since World War II, there's been a striking amount of parental interest in early childhood development. Dr. Michael Lewis, a researcher in child development and professor of pediatrics, psychology and psychiatry at Rutgers University Medical School, says, "As family size has declined, there has been a greater and greater parental investment in each child, and I don't see that changing soon."

Why should this be?

For one thing, with fewer children, parents have more time to devote to each child. Also, better informed, better educated parents are becoming more sensitive to the need to prepare their youngsters for an increasingly complex society. As Barbara Bowman, a child development authority with the Erikson Institute in Chicago, puts it, "They're so anxious that their kids not be left behind, there's almost a hysteria connected with it."

So, according to one recent news report, you find one single mother in California working two jobs so that she can provide swimming lessons and educational toys for her 22-month-old daughter. In a Boston suburb, a married couple has gone even further with their three-year-old son. The mother explains, "You have to start them young and push them on toward their goal. They have to be aware of everything—the alphabet, numbers, reading. I want to fill these little sponges as soon as possible."

Does any of this early, hyped-up, high-pressure instruction and conditioning of children do any good?

There's no doubt that programs for economically disadvantaged youngsters, such as the Head Start Program, have done wonders for children aged three to five. But these children are from homes where they've received very little cultural support. If you try to transfer this approach to children who are *not* disadvantaged, the benefits of this early pressure and education are not so obvious.

According to a number of experts, it's questionable whether there are any real benefits to pushing your child to reach high levels of intellectual or athletic achievement at such early ages. Take the issue of infant swimming. The American Academy of Pediatrics has said, "Although it may be possible to teach young infants to propel themselves and keep their heads above water, infants cannot be expected to learn the elements of water safety or to react appropriately in emergencies. No child, particularly those who are preschool age, can ever be considered 'water safe.'"

Also, there may be dangers if a child, driven by an ambitious mother or father, gets started too early in intense athletic activity. Lawrence Galton points out in his book, *Your Child in Sports*, "If concentrated instruction starts too early, the child whose motor ability is not yet advanced enough often becomes frustrated and gives up."

There also may be physical problems. A few of the dangers that have been noted include:

- Lifting weights or engaging in strenuous gymnastics can injure the spinal column in children who are entering puberty.
- Female ice skaters, ballet dancers and gymnasts may fail to develop normal menstrual cycles because of the pressures on them to keep their weight down.

- Distance running before the early teen years can damage leg bones.
- Children of any age, but particularly those in the preschool or early school years, may suffer serious repercussions from social isolation if they are required to practice any activity for several hours daily.

With this last point, the implications for developing good relationships with a peer group are obvious. If you get your child overly committed to tennis, music lessons or any other discipline at a very young age, that will mean he'll have less time to mix and mingle with other boys and girls his age. As a result, he may develop the particular skill you've chosen for him, but he may *not* develop many all-important social skills that can be just as important to his later self-confidence and success.

Of course, none of this is to say that you shouldn't give your child every opportunity to develop his talents and to strengthen his body and mind. It's just a matter of being sure, as an attentive parent, that it's your *child* who is motivated to play or engage in a certain activity, and not just you. Developing new skills must be an exciting, enjoyable experience for young ones, not a great burden that is being forced by pushy parents. Children who feel coerced will become bored, sulky or contrary—not self-confident.

Of course, you should give your child every encouragement, especially when she evinces a special interest in some field or activity. "One of the most exciting developments in the whole field of psychology," says Dr. Edward Zigler, Sterling Professor of Psychology at Yale, "is our new understanding of the great ability of the infant to learn."

But Zigler, one of the guiding lights of the Head Start Program, goes on to say, "Children learn for the same reason that birds fly. They're programmed to learn, and they do it beautifully. You can't stop children from learning—and you certainly don't have to push them to."

Moreover, Zigler concludes, "The idea that by the age of three you can get on the track for Harvard is absurd. As a parent, if you just take your time and wait until your children get to school, by the age of ten, you will not know the difference between your child and one who has been instructed earlier."

In the last analysis, it's all a matter of balance. Remember: As your children move through the later preschool and early elementary school years, their intellectual and athletic skills can certainly be sharpened. But all of this must be done in a context of love and warmth, and not pushiness. If you start pressing your child to achieve intellectual goals or reach athletic peaks, your efforts are almost certain to backfire. It's very likely that your child will quickly react negatively to everything you're trying to get him to do. He won't be at all interested in the intellectual or athletic pursuits that you've laid out for him. Most important of all, you will have robbed him of important time that he might have used learning to cooperate and interact effectively with his peers.

Dr. John H. Flavell, Professor of Psychology at Stanford University, puts it this way: "Children have important cognitive things to learn in these early years that have nothing to do with school—like learning how other people feel."

That great sage of child rearing, Dr. Benjamin Spock, observes, "I worry that these kids will be over-intellectualized. Being persuaded that the most important thing is to be bright and get good grades may move people away from the natural, emotional ways of dealing with life."

If youngsters are "over-intellectualized" or over-athleticized, the result can be a severe threat to their self-confidence. They certainly won't feel good about themselves or the skills that their parents may be pressing them to develop. Instead, they may become timid, isolated loners who have no idea how to make sense out of life or find satisfaction in the company of others.

To sum up, the main messages for parents whose children have entered the fourth self-confidence crisis of peer interaction and competition are these:

1. Give your child at an early age every opportunity to develop his physical and intellectual potential.
2. Let your youngster take risks and teach her to keep trying, even when she fails in her first efforts. An ability to overcome failure and survive setbacks can be one of the most significant qualities leading to self-confidence and success.
3. Allow her to develop her potential naturally, at her own pace.

4. Provide him with constant reassurances that you love him, whatever his degree of achievement.

5. Finally, remember that the social skills your child is developing from about age three onward will be just as important for her self-confidence and success as her individual talents. So pay as much attention to nurturing those social abilities—the "team temperament"—as you do to individual achievements.

With this approach, your child will still have every chance of becoming a star on the playing field or the brightest kid in the classroom. But at the same time, he'll be in the strongest position to develop a healthy sense of self-respect and self-confidence—qualities that will make him a happier and more satisfied individual, whatever his level of achievement.

8

Crisis Five:
The
Wars of
Independence

Independence. That's ultimately what developing self-confidence in childhood is all about: acquiring the ability to function in life as an independent, self-assured, self-starting, achievement-oriented adult.

Up to this point, we've been discussing how the seeds of self-confidence are first planted. As they begin to grow your child learns to interact and collaborate with his peers. But during this entire process, an ongoing, widening separation is taking place between the two of you. Your ultimate goal, as wrenching as it may be, is to help that offspring of yours to strengthen her wings, spread them to their full span—and finally, take flight. In short, your ultimate goal is an empty nest.

But it's not easy to prepare sons and daughters to operate effectively on their own. For one thing, there will be plenty of false starts, painful breaks and stresses, and strains on your relationship. Also, it's profoundly sad to see that little one grow up, begin to order his own life and eventually reach the point where he no longer seems to need you.

In the last analysis, however, independence is the ultimate objective. Unless your youngster can begin to function effectively apart from you, he'll never be able to reach his full potential in life. And the only way he can hope to achieve that potential is to put the finishing touches on the core of self-confidence that you've been working so hard to give him.

It's helpful to think of this final phase in the development of self-confidence in terms of successfully meeting several major challenges, including:

1. going to school;
2. establishing independent disciplines and standards for achievement;
3. making it through adolescence; and
4. possibly sustaining the blow of parents' divorce.

Obviously, there are many other challenges a child will face as he grows older and becomes increasingly independent of his parents. But learning to deal with these representative difficulties will give children and parents the coping techniques they need to achieve a healthy "emptying of the nest."

The goal is to enable a youngster to emerge from such challenges with his self-confidence not only intact, but stronger for the experience. Then, he should be ready to withstand almost anything else the world has to offer.

CHALLENGE #1: GOING TO SCHOOL

Any separation—whether the result of going to school, being exposed to parents' divorce or the death of a loved one—can have a wrenching impact on a youngster's self-confidence.

As far as school is concerned, Melvin Lewis, an eminent authority in the child education field, says there are two major ingredients for a successful transition from home to nursery school—the most common form of separation for a three-year-old. These are:

1. First, the youngster needs a solid "secondary attachment figure"—in most cases, a teacher who is supportive and, preferably, familiar to the child. For this reason, preliminary visits by the child to the school before the school year begins are very important.

2.   Secondly, the child needs to know where his mother is and feel reassured that she will return at some predictable point to pick him up.

This second factor ties in quite closely with what Dr. Burton White and other experts have pointed out as an impulse toward greater separation from parents that occurs around age three. You'll recall that infants are often willing to explore their environment so long as they can hear their mother's voice. They may also need to see her from the next room and return to her periodically after short intervals.

With the three- or four-year-old, longer separations are in order. But still, the preschooler must know in his head that Mommy is in some predictable place and will be coming back at a predictable time. Certainly, the child has no real time sense at the age of three. But he needs to have the assurance that the parents will pick him up after his school activity is finished.

Of course, this next phase of separation from the parent doesn't necessarily come automatically. In many cases, the child has to be prepared. Otherwise, he may resist going to school on a regular basis, and the situation may get worse as the nursery school year wears on.

So what should you do to prepare your youngster for this first major step of independence? There are two phases of preparation.

Preparation for Separation—Phase One:

First, as far as nursery school is concerned, don't even try to take your child to school if he feels sick or is really upset about something. This is not "spoiling" him. Rather, by exercising a little flexibility, you'll help him make the transition from home to school much more easily.

Of course, *every* child resists going to school or other group programs at one time or another. In most cases, this resistance is nothing more than an expression of inertia, laziness or an attempt to control the parent in some way. So most of the time, it's enough just to be sympathetic with the child's early morning crankiness and then lead him gently out of the door and toward the school. Usually, the youngster's mood will change as soon as he gets a few steps out of the house.

On the other hand, it's important to determine whether the child really is sick, or something serious is bothering him about school or some other aspect of his life. In such a case, you'll be well advised to straighten that out before you push him into a classroom.

But don't misunderstand what I'm saying: It won't do a thing for a child's self-confidence to teach him that every time he makes a scene, he can succeed in getting a particular activity cancelled. That's teaching him *manipulation*, rather than healthy self-confidence!

I'm reminded of one weepy boy who demanded that his mother remain with him in nursery school every day for much longer than the other mothers. Later, he was placed in a special art class, but his mother agreed to take him out after he had raised just one protest. The same thing happened when he was enrolled in a local music class.

On one level, I suppose you could say that the child became confident that he could control his mother quite effectively with these resisting techniques. But he was also learning that he didn't have to stick with a project once he started it. Also, he was *failing* to learn good coping patterns when he confronted new learning challenges and new groups of peers.

So it's essential, as you work with your child during this transition period to greater independence, that you make an important distinction: You must distinguish between loving concern and flexibility on the one hand, and communicating the idea that it's always all right to back out of a commitment on the other. You can also minimize problems by carefully assessing your child's readiness for a program. Bonnie enjoyed somersaults and cartwheels on our lawn long before she was ready for the discipline of tumbling lessons.

A large part of a child's healthy separation from parents during the early nursery school and school years is learning to operate on his own, with growing degrees of staying power. You'll undercut the development of this healthy kind of independence if you give in too quickly when your child complains about joining in some activity.

Preparation for Separation—Phase Two:

Second, try to maintain a calm atmosphere in the home in the morning, just before you leave for the educational program. Often, this means it's wise to make some preparations the night before, such as laying out clothes and school supplies. That way, you can get your youngster out of the door with a minimum of pressure.

Sometimes, though, it's not possible to do everything the night before: you'll find that you just can't always get everything together in absolutely perfect order before the time to leave arrives. When the pressure is really on, I'd suggest that you err on the side of keeping your child relaxed and happy before the departure. This approach is far preferable to achieving perfect preparation.

For example, your youngster may insist on wearing an outfit that isn't exactly what you had in mind—perhaps the shirt and pants don't match. You can always get into a big argument and impose your will on the youngster. But the result may be an emotional scene which ruins the child's whole school day.

In such a case, the main issue is not the clothes: It's the emotional condition of your family. You want to try to send your child off feeling good about himself and good about the world. Then, he'll be much more likely to have a positive experience when he gets to school.

I learned this through trial and error with my own daughter, Bonnie. After a couple of missteps, I discovered that if I waited to dress Bonnie until after breakfast, we'd both be under far too much pressure just before we left for the nursery school. Breakfast in our home is always stretched out longer than I plan. As a result, if we eat first, we have far too little time for the dressing and other final preparations. When Bonnie was smaller, major battles would result, and I'd end up taking her off to school while we were both angry at each other. It was during that time of her life that she was particularly attached to her security blanket—and now I can understand why!

So before long, I learned to dress her as soon as she got up. That way, we could enjoy some more relaxed time together, eat a leisurely breakfast, and then head off to her nursery school program in a more serene frame of mind. Of course, the price I paid for that calm is that sometimes her carefully combed hair would get messed up. Also, she might have some stains on her shirt from spilling her apple juice. But at least she would arrive at the nursery school in good spirits.

In this regard, I'm reminded of a story I heard about a mother who impressed all the other mothers at school because her five children always seemed to arrive on time and in the best of humor. It was true that their clothes often seemed a little too wrinkled, but that was far outweighed by the children's sunny moods.

Her secret, which she finally confessed to one of the other parents, was that she dressed the children the night before and let them sleep with their school clothes on!

There was just no way that she could get five children put together in the morning and out on time without a Herculean effort the night before. She reasoned that their clothes were going to get wrinkled anyhow after a couple of hours. So she decided that to start them off a little wrinkled was not all that bad.

So at the beginning of the school experience, you should try to make the preparation period and trip to school as smooth and pleasurable as possible. That way, your child is much more likely to get off on the right foot in adjusting to separation from you—and learning to operate in an assured, confident way in an educational setting.

Selecting a School for Your Child

But what happens after the child arrives at school? You can never be sure what kind of a nursery situation you're getting your child into until you examine it. For this reason, I'd suggest spending some time talking with the teachers and also observing at least part of one of the sessions. If you discover that parents are not wanted in a school that you're considering, I'd take that as a signal that that's not the place for your child.

In general, I'd suggest these four guidelines to keep in mind when you're trying to find a school that's going to be best for your child.

Guideline #1: Before enrolling your child, talk to some parents who have children in that particular class. Ask their opinion of the headmistress and other instructors.

Guideline #2: Talk at length with the headmistress about her philosophy of child care—especially her approach to discipline and her feelings about security blankets. If she seems too rigid about wanting the children to behave like "little adults" I'd stay away from the place.

One little girl who was attending a particular preschool program was especially tired one morning when she entered class. As a result, she was very "clingy," and her parents decided to allow her to take her security blanket with her in case she wanted it with her when she took a nap.

Enter "the villain" in the person of the woman who was in charge of caring for the children. The moment she saw the security blanket, she confiscated it—despite the three-year-old's tears. Moreover, she refused to return it, even though the child continued to wail.

Fortunately, the father who had dropped the child off decided to circle back and double-check how the youngster was doing in the class. He was particularly concerned because he knew she had been in a bad mood when she had arrived. When he returned, he found the girl upset and crying. And the caretaker made no secret of her position: "It's not appropriate for a child of Judy's age to still be carrying around a security blanket," she declared.

The father, quite understandably, immediately took the little girl out of the class, and the parents began to look for a new nursery school.

Of course, this kind of attitude is not limited to nursery schools. I had a somewhat similar experience with rigidity when I was considering a swimming program for my daughter. As I was questioning the instructor, she gave what seemed to me to be all the correct answers. But I was somewhat troubled by what I perceived as an underlying sternness in her.

So I asked: "What do you do with the two-year-old who won't perform specific activities at a given time?"

Her no-nonsense response: "Well, they *do* it!"

"Now, wait a minute," I said. "Once in a while, you must have a child who, for whatever reason, on that particular day just doesn't want to cooperate in that activity."

Her attitude just wasn't acceptable to me: "Well, as far as I'm concerned, then she can just leave."

Obviously, she resented the idea that I would even suggest a two-year-old might not always be cooperative. Also, my direct questions probably threatened her somewhat. But if I could threaten her or make her angry by asking some rather innocuous questions, how angry might a two-year-old make her? And as you know if you have one, two-year-olds *can* make you *very* angry!

Although I'm confident that this woman could have taught Bonnie how to swim, her expertise was not at issue. I felt that she just wasn't sufficiently attuned to potential problems that might arise with younger children, and so I decided not to trust her with my child.

Guideline #3:   You should be entitled to an hour's visit to the class itself—at a minimum. So take advantage of this opportunity to observe how the instructors handle the children and whether any of the youngsters are allowed to use their security blankets, pacifiers or other personal "self-confidence" equipment.

Remember: These early classes are mostly a time of transition for your child from the familiar, warm environment of the home to the outside world. If the change is too abrupt or threatening, children may come to believe that the outside world is mostly an inhospitable place where they won't be happy. In fact, they may begin to think that they can't function effectively in a situation where they're separate from their parents. This kind of message to a child can deal a serious blow to the development of solid self-confidence.

Guideline #4:   Finally, do the instructors in the educational program get down on their *hands and knees* to interact with the children?

This may seem a little odd, but I consider it to be very important. Let me explain. What you want in a transitional educational setting is an environment where your child can develop greater self-confidence by learning that he can influence his environment beyond the home. One way to convey this message is for the instructor to get down on the floor, on the child's level, and communicate directly with the child on a more equal basis.

No matter how self-confident or assured a preschooler may seem, all an adult has to do is to speak loudly and sternly from a towering standing position, and that childish veneer of assurance will immediately melt away. Sometimes, of course, when a child disobeys, breaks rules or behaves disruptively, it's necessary to project the image of the decisive, towering adult. But for most of the day, it's much more helpful to foster a friendlier environment where the youngster can be himself and believe that he's being accepted completely by the adult in charge. And the best way to do this is to interact on the floor.

Many child psychology books will tell you that the most fascinating thing for an infant, toddler or preschooler is the adult who happens to be in charge of him at the moment. The *adult's* reaction to him is far more stimulating and important than his contact with any of his toys. And learning how to communicate with and even influence the adult can be one of the most important sources of self-confidence at this age.

It's easy to see how learning self-confidence on the toddler's level can develop into confidence as an adult. A great part of self-confidence is believing that when you deal with people in authority, you have a chance of getting a positive response. For example, if you're a prospective employer and I'm self-confident when I go in for an interview with you, you'll be more likely to respond positively to me and perhaps give me the job. On the other hand, if I go in feeling timid and insecure, that's also going to be communicated to you, with a greater likelihood of a negative result.

Still, having a sense of assurance that you can influence people to feel more positively toward you is only part of the story. Another important element in self-confidence is the ability to relate to and understand the reactions of other people, even when they don't react positively to you.

In other words, it's important to recognize that negative reactions are not necessarily the result of anything you've done or some inadequacy in your own personal makeup. In short, you don't have to take the blame for negative responses in many cases. A firm sense of self-confidence will give you a better perspective on how to deal with rejection.

So, to summarize, playing and responding on the floor with a child will accomplish a number of things:

- He'll realize that he can get a positive response from other adults besides his parents and other caretakers.
- He'll learn *how* to get that positive response. If he smiles or does something cute, the other person should laugh. If he moves some toy, the other person should react in some appropriate way.
- He'll get in the habit of *practicing* getting those positive responses—usually, long after the adult has tired of the game.
- Your youngster will learn to *understand* better how the adult mind works if his interaction with adults is close and intense. And the better he understands, the better he'll comprehend why certain people behave toward him in the way they do.

It's never too early to begin to learn *why* others are treating us in the way they are. The sooner we begin to discern motives and personality differences in others, the sooner we can distance ourselves from their negative reactions to us. Before long, we learn to treat their rejections, as well as their acceptances, more objectively.

One other important consideration in choosing a nursery school: If licensing is required by your state or community, be sure to check the status of the schools you're considering. In New York City, for example, the Municipal Division of Day Care in the Department of Health enforces health code regulations covering nursery schools. This agency stipulates that the teachers must be licensed either by the city or certified by the state. Also, children must have regular physicals.

There have been several scandals involving child-care facilities, including some related to sexual abuse, so parents must be wary. Even after you've selected a school that may seem perfect in every way, you should listen carefully to what your children report back to you. Then, act immediately if you sense something is wrong with the teachers or the environment.

As your child gets older, he'll be staying away from you for longer and longer periods of time in a school setting. When the time to enter first grade arrives, your child is moving beyond the transition phase. He has embarked on the long-term educational process that will continue through his high school and college years. Mom and Dad won't be around as much to monitor what is going on in the school. So it's very important that in the very early years, the youngster have a solid foundation of healthy, positive separation to build upon.

Those early, preschool educational experiences, as short as they may be—with the parent often at hand when the situation requires it—are crucial in helping your child become confident in working with adult teachers and childhood peers. The time you take beginning in toddlerhood will pay huge dividends in your youngster's later self-confidence, both in helping him relate to his schoolmates and also achieve his maximum success in schoolwork.

CHALLENGE #2: ESTABLISHING INDEPENDENT DISCIPLINES AND STANDARDS FOR ACHIEVEMENT

Children really begin to "show the stuff" of their self-confidence when they start pursuing independent work assignments in school and later independent responsibilities in jobs. When a child is put in the position of having to perform in these areas, apart from parental supervision and guidance, the level of self-confidence can spell the difference between mediocre and high achievement, or even between success and failure.

To enable your child to become effective in these independent projects, it's necessary to help her establish independent disciplines and standards for achievement. And one of the greatest proving grounds for encouraging this sort of independence involves the issue of homework.

These days, you'll probably find that your child begins to get homework assignments as early as the first grade, or perhaps even earlier in some special schools. Typically, the emphasis is on the child's developing the ability to become a self-starter and accomplish his own assignments with as little outside help as possible. Yet various studies have shown that parental participation can be significant in helping a child become an academic success.

Professor Herbert Walberg, of the University of Illinois at Chicago, reviewed more than 2,500 studies on elements that lead to a youngster's success in schoolwork. He found that parental participation in homework with children was much more important for the child's achievement levels than were ethnic, racial or economic backgrounds.

What did Dr. Walberg find that parents did to help their children? Among the most effective forms of assistance, he said, were:

- talking about school activities;
- encouraging leisure reading;
- limiting television time;
- taking youngsters on educational trips; and
- in general, showing affection and interest in the child's welfare.

Such attitudes and behaviors, Dr. Walberg says, can result in as much as a 50 percent increase in grades and test scores among students.

Research by Dr. Walberg and others has indicated that homework that is evaluated or commented upon has three times more effect on a student's achievement than does the youngster's social and economic background. On the other hand, homework done *without* any adult feedback has little or no effect on achievement levels.*

* Education Supplement, *The New York Times*, November 9, 1986.

Amitai Etzioni, a George Washington University sociologist, puts it well when he says: "Homework can be an effective means of instilling self-discipline and helping a child improve his achievement if it is meaningfully and fairly evaluated."

What does all this have to say about you, as a parent who is interested in instilling independence, discipline and high standards of achievement in her youngster?

Clearly, as a child embarks on more independent ventures in schoolwork or other important activities, it's important for the parents to play an active role in the child's transition from dependence on the family to independence. Parents who guide and advise their children are much more likely to see their youngsters achieving more and also exhibiting greater self-confidence in their outside activities.

In a way, this parental participation is an instruction period that allows the parents to pass on important information and techniques about how to operate effectively and successfully in the outside world. Without this parental guidance, the child must learn by hit and miss, trial and error, and that's not a very good or efficient way to excel or reach one's potential in an optimum amount of time. Eventually, of course, your child will begin to depend less and less on you, and finally, he'll be operating pretty much on his own. But you should expect to have a significant influence during that transition time when he's learning what it really means to be independent.

CHALLENGE #3: MAKING IT THROUGH ADOLESCENCE

Contrary to many common beliefs, adolescents, on the whole, are not obnoxious, antisocial or rebellious. In fact, only about 20 percent of all adolescents are severely emotionally disturbed, according to studies by Daniel Offer, the head of the psychiatry department at Michael Reese Hospital in Chicago. Dr. Reese has also reported that the large majority of teenagers are *not* in rebellion against their families and enjoy a smooth transition from childhood to adulthood.

Still, as every parent of an adolescent knows, there can be stresses and strains in family relationships as a youngster goes through this final stage of independence from parental authority. One major characteristic of this phase is teenage silence around parents, observes Dr. Leonard D. Eron, a professor of psychology at the University of Illinois in Chicago. This "silent treatment," which characterizes many children between the ages of 12 and 15, doesn't reflect a lack of love on the part of the youngsters toward their parents. Rather, it's an adolescent's way of asserting independence and a right to privacy—and also a way of exhibiting self-confidence. According to the experts, several specific factors may be responsible for the silent treatment:

- Youngsters don't want to talk about the body changes they are experiencing as they move toward adulthood, Dr. Freda Rebelsky, a professor of psychology at Boston University, explains. Sometimes, the children are embarrassed to talk about these changes; other times, they just don't have the knowledge to discuss them intelligently, so they keep their mouths shut.
- Teenagers want to be more independent of their parents, and not talking "is a way of establishing some separation," according to Dr. Anne C. Petersen, a professor at Pennsylvania State University.
- Silence can give adolescents a feeling of control over their lives when the changes that are occurring in them make everything seem out of control. In a 1986 survey in *TeenAge* magazine, 47 percent of American teenagers said they had total control over their lives, while 52 percent said they had "some" control. Only 1 percent said they had no control. Any tensions between parents and teenage children, including refusals by a child to talk very much, just reflect this shift from some to total control that occurs as we move from childhood to adulthood.
- Many adolescents are intensely involved in exploring their individuality, and many times, they want to make decisions without any input or advice from their parents.

In general, the bases of the foundations for a child's self-confidence have been laid before adolescence arrives. What you see during the teenage years is the playing out of the influences and developments that have gone before. In most cases, if a child has been encouraged to be self-confident and have a high sense of self-esteem, that self-confidence and self-esteem will blossom during the teenage years and come into full flower in adulthood.

But still, parents can undercut feelings of self-confidence among teenagers if they fail to remain sensitive to the youngster's needs and natural process of development and separation from the family. One of the most devastating events that can wreak havoc on self-confidence during adolescence—or at any other time of a child's life, for that matter—is divorce.

CHALLENGE #4: SURVIVING THE BLOW OF PARENTS' DIVORCE

Divorce can deal a devastating blow to a child's self-confidence. Unfortunately, the divorce rate seems to be increasing. Each year, the parents of one million children will become divorced. In fact, if present trends continue, census reports indicate that two in five children born in the mid-1980s run the risk of family divorce—and one in five will experience a *second* divorce.

So what can be done about this problem?

Be honest and realistic. There is more involved than just you and your own happiness, or what you perceive as your happiness. One of the reasons that marriage has been handed down to us, by ideal definitions, as a *permanent* relationship is the confirmation over the centuries of the importance of a stable family.

And that means stability not just for the adults, but for the children as well. When you kick the props out from under a youngster through a divorce proceeding, that child's emotional stability will definitely suffer—and his self-confidence will plummet.

The evidence on the deleterious impact of divorce on children has been piling up in recent studies conducted throughout the country. At one school in Michigan, a psychiatrist observed that several children of divorce "became noisy, possessive and restless, pushing, kicking, hitting and even occasionally biting their classmates."

Another psychiatrist, Dr. Barry D. Garfinkel, has analyzed youthful suicide attempts at Bradley Hospital in East Providence, Rhode Island. In this seven-year, 500-case study published in *The American Journal of Psychiatry*, Dr. Garfinkel said, "More than half of the families had an absent parent. In a quarter of them, both parents were absent. It really stresses the need for communication with an adult."

Children whose parents have been divorced often just don't know who they are. Also, they tend to fall down in classwork and achieve at much lower levels than those with intact families.

"The accelerating divorce rate in the United States has closely paralleled the rise in drug use," Dr. Armand M. Nicholi, Jr., wrote in the *New England Journal of Medicine*. "Moreover, poor academic performance, susceptibility to peer influence and delinquent behavior (all characteristic of drug users), as well as suicide and homicide, have been found to be more pronounced among children from homes with one or both parents missing or frequently absent."

A variety of other recent studies show clearly that divorce destroys a youngster's confidence not only in his home life and in his parents, but most crippling of all, in himself. Consider this sampling:

- A study at Kent State University in Ohio confirmed that girls do weather the divorce crisis better than boys. But this report said that the children from "together" families fare better than *all* of those from homes of divorce, whether boys or girls. As something of a consolation to those who must divorce, the children of divorce who were able to maintain meaningful contacts with both parents adjusted better than those who had a relationship with only one parent.
- Another study by the National Association of Elementary School Principals revealed higher rates of tardiness, truancy and expulsion among children being reared by only one parent.
- The landmark California Children of Divorce Study, a 10-year project that was the longest of its kind, found that even in their late teens and early maturity, some children of divorce were virtually devoid of self-confidence. They feared betrayal and worried that their relationships with others would prove unreliable.

A young woman interviewed for this study said, "Every time my boyfriend is 30 minutes late, I think he's with another woman."

A young man: "I saw my dad beat up my mom. That is a scar I think of every day."

A 19-year-old youth: "The hardest thing for me was my mother's pain. I remember the night when my dad left and how my mom sat up all night rocking and crying in the red rocking chair, and I cried, too."

This California study also found that preschoolers tended to be most upset by a parental breakup. They especially feared that both their parents would leave them. Even five years after the divorce, more than a third of these children suffered moderate to severe depression. On a more positive note, a decade after the divorce none mentioned being as frightened as they had been at the time of the breakup.

One of the saddest and most poignant reactions reported in this study was the typical fantasy that the children had that their parents would remarry. Terry, who was three at the time of the divorce, said, "I wish my stepfather would go back to his first wife. I wish my stepmother would go back to her first husband. I would like my mom and dad to get back together again."

A number of children in their early teens wrote to their fathers who had left them, sending emotional messages and lines of poetry. Even though these children might only see their fathers once a year, they stubbornly pictured them as loving parents.

Clearly, the children of divorce face a no-win situation. So what should you as a parent do to combat this situation and protect your child's self-confidence? Dr. Judith S. Wallerstein, the principle investigator in the California study, and author Joan Berlin Kelly, offer a couple of good, succinct suggestions for damage control.

Strategy #1

Parents should avoid fooling themselves about the impact of divorce on their children. Don't make the comfortable mistake of hoping that the youngsters "will just get over it." Instead, act as swiftly as possible to resolve any conflicts that you may be facing and *avoid* that divorce!

Strategy #2

If divorce is inevitable, understand that your youngsters will do better when they're allowed to maintain relationships with *both* parents. Children who are prevented from carrying on a relationship with either a mother or father are more likely to feel rejected—and their sense of self worth will decline commensurately.

Obviously, I think there's a lot to be said for that "outdated" concept: keeping families intact for the sake of the children. A number of studies have indicated that families in which the parents are fighting all the time are certainly not good for the development of a child's self confidence or emotional stability. At the same time, there is some evidence that even a fighting family may be better than one in which the parents are divorced.

But even as I urge you to resolve your differences and stay together so that your children can develop to their full potential, I'm also realistic. I know that we're facing a huge, accelerating divorce rate, with more than half of the marriages in this country ending in divorce. So it's necessary to know specifically what to do if divorce seems inevitable in your situation. You might keep these four steps in mind as you're thinking of ways to prepare your children for a marital split.

Step 1: Break the news to them as gently as possible, *without* laying the blame for the breakup on either parent. This is best done by both parents together, showing that you can still cooperate on matters important to the children.

Step 2: Reassure the youngsters that they will *always* have a home life with either the father or mother. But emphasize that whomever they live with, the other parent will welcome them on long and frequent visits.

Step 3: Refrain from insisting that they "choose sides" in the family fight. Also, where appropriate, allow them to decide in which home they would prefer to live, and do this without making them feel guilty about their decision. After all, if you don't do this, the court may do it for you.

Step 4: Fathers, don't desert your children—and especially your sons—after the breakup!

According to a study in the *New England Journal of Medicine*, two months after a divorce, less than half the fathers were meeting their children weekly. Three years later, half of them weren't seeing the children at all.

Don't neglect your children after you leave home. If you do, you may find yourself in the position of one alcoholic father who learned that his son had toured neighborhood bars for years in search of him.

Also, don't subject yourself to the anguish of the disc jockey whose son hitchhiked from Boston to Minneapolis to see his father, though he hadn't heard from him since he was three years old. Unfortunately, in this case, the boy's mission failed.

"I just wanted to meet him, you know, and tell him the kind of music I like," the boy explained. "But I couldn't find him in the phone book, so I gave up and came home. I guess I really chickened out."

For a child, there can be no happy ending with a divorce. But at least the blow may be softened and the child's self-confidence bolstered somewhat by sensitive parents who think enough of their children to sacrifice a little of their self-realization.

9

Parents
Need
Self-Confidence
Too

It's a cruel irony: Parents have never been so devoted to their children or so involved in child rearing as they are today; yet they seem more confused and uncertain than ever. In short, despite the Niagara of advice that pours over them daily in books, magazines, newspaper columns and the electronic media, they lack the very essence of effective parenthood—self-confidence. And unfortunately, an un-self-confident parent often breeds an un-self-confident child.

Being aware of this problem, I wanted to set a good example for both my youngsters—and my starting point was one of my own problems, a fear of dogs. Soon, I got my chance. One day, when Keith was looking out of the window, he saw our neighbor walking his poodle, Muffin. So Keith said, "Want to say hello to Muffin." But I hesitated. All I could think of were those bad experiences I'd had and how nervous I was around dogs.

Keith, I realized, would have his own closetful of insecurities someday as a result of his own experiences. It really wasn't fair to add my problems to his collection as well! So I screwed up my courage, and we went outside. And thank goodness, Muffin was on a leash!

Of course, no matter how much courage we may display in forcing ourselves into a threatening situation, our fears may get communicated. I wonder how much Keith and Bonnie have picked up my fear of dogs—even though I try not to display these feelings around the youngsters. On the other hand, I may succeed too well and they'll want dogs of their own!

In short, no matter how much you try to teach your children about self-confidence and how supportive an environment you try to build in the home, the greatest influence on your youngster's sense of self-confidence is going to be *you*. So it's extremely important to monitor very closely the unspoken messages that you're communicating to your children about security, self-worth and personal assurance.

One subconscious trap that affects many families, and prevents children from developing adequate self-confidence, is an adult tendency to undermine the child's self-confidence because the adult himself feels threatened. Sometimes, we mothers and fathers have unmet needs and problems that we're wrestling with, and we may try to resolve those concerns or push them aside when we're dealing with our children. We forget that our youngsters are always dependent on us for direction, guidelines and evaluations of what they can and cannot do.

For example, if a father comes home after a bad day at the office with pent-up emotions that he hasn't been able to express during the day, he may lash out at his wife and children.

Is this really fair? Of course it's not! Yet it happens all the time, day in and day out in American homes. And these days, when many families have two working spouses, *both* may lash out at the children, as well as at each other, out of unresolved frustration. Such "acting out" on the part of parents may make them feel better, but such reactions don't do a thing for a child's emotional development and self-confidence.

Another way that parents' own lack of self-confidence may sneak up and sabotage the self-confidence of a child is in the area of basic beliefs, values and worldviews. The Harvard child psychologist Robert Coles put it this way in an interview with *U.S. News & World Report*:

Many parents are afraid to bring up their children on their own—with their own convictions and their own moral faith. They're intimidated by all these experts who write books about child rearing and tell them what to do. This is partially because parents have abdicated a higher vision, whether it be religious or political, and they no longer believe, really, in a national purpose. Having turned away from both God and country, they are left with themselves—and their own comforts.

For 15 or 20 years now, when I have asked American people what they believe in, they have said, "I believe in my children." Now, when children have become a source of almost idolatrous religious faith this is quite a burden for children to bear. Parents forget that what children need perhaps more than anything is discipline and a sense of commitment to something larger than themselves. Children need to be asked of, as well as given to.

So parents, as well as children, are facing a self-confidence crisis. And the children may suffer even more than the parents unless the adults start getting their acts together!

But what's a parent to do? How can you begin to tackle this problem of your own self-confidence—and then project an improved sense of self-worth to your offspring?

Rather than trying to wrestle with the problem of parental self-confidence as one enormous concept, I prefer to break it down into various component parts. These components of parental self-confidence tend to fall into specialized "confidence areas" that must first be dealt with individually. Then, when you put them all together, you are more likely to end up with a parental image that will inspire greater self-confidence in your children.

THE CONFIDENCE OF VALUES

We live in an age of relativism, in which one belief is often held to be as valid as another. Unfortunately, this often results in parents believing nothing at all, and passing down this lack of belief to their children.

In the past, strong, stable families were rooted in religious, national and community values that made relationships and morality much more fixed and predictable. Children were brought up to know what was right and wrong: If they violated the prevailing moral order, they knew it!

In our culture, in contrast, the foundations of moral and spiritual values have crumbled. Parents don't automatically affirm a given belief system; there's no pressure whatsoever to do so. Instead, *they* must choose what's right or wrong. Usually, there's no one else to help them decide. The community pressures that existed in the past to believe or behave in a certain way have largely disappeared. Now it's up to the individual to decide what to believe in and how to behave.

Unfortunately, however, many individuals, including many parents, often *don't* decide. Instead, they remain uncommitted. What such parents communicate to their children is that there is no ethical basis for taking moral action. In other words, there's no way that you can be *confident* that certain actions are right and certain actions are wrong.

Moreover, even if a parent states unequivocally that something is right or wrong, he's usually unable to say *why* it's right or wrong. There's no coherent worldview. If parents believe in God—and a large majority of Americans certainly do—the precise way that the deity and religious values relate to the individual may remain a mystery to them and will probably be passed on as a mystery to their youngsters.

So my message to parents is this: Take a stand! Explore this whole issue of spiritual and moral values and make a decision about what you believe! If you can't decide, you can't expect your children to. The result will be youngsters who grow up without any firm reference point about basic values, and who are forced to enter the adult world without one of the most important ingredients of self-confidence.

THE CONFIDENCE OF DISCIPLINE

I happened to be visiting a friend when she was giving her two-year-old son a bath. Suddenly, as is not uncommon with children that age, the boy bit her. Without hesitation, she bit him back. Then she explained proudly to me, "That should do it. Now he knows how I feel when he bites me!"

Was she right? Absolutely not!

At that age, a child simply cannot understand fully the consequences of his actions. Before the age of about four, there are certain things that a child is just not capable of comprehending, and one of them is why others react as they do.

How to administer discipline is certainly not easy to master.

Among other things, we mustn't assume that in imposing punishment we can communicate an adult message to a child, because the child simply isn't ready for it. Still, in my opinion, a parent can feel self-confident about her disciplinary measures—and exorcise those nagging doubts about whether she is doing "the right thing"—if she follows three simple rules:

First, she must be prompt in inflicting punishment. Do it as soon as possible after the transgression.

Second, she must be consistent in administering punishment. In other words, if your child "talks back" on one occasion and you send him to his room, use the same or similar disciplinary measure the next time. Don't just ignore it. Otherwise, he'll be getting mixed signals.

Third, the parent must be firm in carrying through with punishment, despite the sobs and howls of the youngster. If a child discovers that he can delay or eliminate punishment by such distracting measures, he may become quite manipulative with the parent—and why not? Wouldn't *you* do everything you could to escape a spanking?

Fourth, make the punishment fit the crime. In particular, it's important not to overreact. We live in an era when a great deal of emphasis has been placed, quite rightly, on combating the scourge of child abuse. Some parents fly off the handle at a minor transgression and beat the children mercilessly—a habit which is far worse than not punishing them at all!

So it's important to keep strict control over the way you administer punishment, especially if you decide to spank or mete out other corporal punishment. Young bodies are very vulnerable. A blow to the head—and I would *always* advise against striking the child in such a vulnerable spot—can do permanent injury.

Children who have been punished too much, just as those who have been disciplined too little, will find that the rules at home somehow don't match those in the real world. As a result, they may never be able to adjust to normal, healthy relationships with their family members, their peers or the all-important authority figures who will exercise great influence over their ultimate destinies.

Fifth, try to build a discipline system that will be relevant in the world outside the family. Teachers, baby-sitters and others should not and usually will not discipline by spanking. If this is all your child responds to, you and he will have a problem.

One effective approach, used by a number of schools, involves a multitiered approach to discipline. In kindergarten, for example, a first offense requires the child to print his own name on the blackboard. For the second offense, he must put a checkmark beside his name. For the third, he "sits out" five minutes of recess time. For the fourth offense, he goes to the principal for a talk. At the end of each day, the slate is literally, as well as figuratively, "wiped clean." I have found a similar set of escalating punishments effective with our children at home.

THE CONFIDENCE OF PATIENCE

Most parents, as well as most other human beings, are impatient. We get into a hurry because we want something right away; or we're afraid someone else won't wait for us if we delay a little bit. Often, we lack confidence that we can move along at a slower pace and still have our lives turn out all right.

But when a parent gets impatient, he can end up demanding far too much from a child. And that can be a serious threat to the development of a youngster's self-confidence.

One three-year-old wanted her mother to tie her shoelaces. But the adult got caught up in a flurry of last-minute preparations to take the girl to nursery school, and she said, "You can tie them yourself!"

What was going through the mother's mind? In part, she was afraid that she might not come across as a responsible parent to the teachers and the other parents if she showed up late. So she put undue pressure on her daughter.

Unfortunately, the little girl could not tie the shoelaces. But she did make an attempt—and ended up wrapping them up into a horrible knot, which caused the mother to lose instead of save time.

I wonder how often, when a child asks for help, the parents have said, "You can do that yourself"—despite the fact that they know that the child really *can't* do it. Sometimes, adults want to buy time for themselves on another project. Other times, they just don't want to be bothered. Or they may feel that just trying, even without a chance of success, is somehow "character building" instead of just frustrating. In any case, they aren't being fair to the child.

Something else that many parents do is get so involved in their own work that they feel that they can't take time away for the "less important" activities of their youngster. So when the child asks them for something they say, "I'll do that for you in just a minute."

But it isn't until age six or seven that a child has any idea of what a minute, an hour, a day or a week really are. To him, the word "minute" simply means rejection! In fact, when one little girl made a request of her mother, she got into the habit of attaching an extra condition: "Don't say minute, Mommy!" Out of the mouths of babes . . .

Many parents often don't appreciate the fact that small children will grasp only gradually the systematic, step-by-step approach that's necessary to complete a complex project. One mother complained to me that her preschooler never finished his attempts at painting a picture in oils. He'd do the background, she said, but then he'd let it go at that.

What she didn't understand was that the boy was too young to complete a relatively long, multi-phase project. First, he would have to do the background. Then, he would have to let this first phase dry before he could tackle the figures. Finally, after the painting had dried further, he could move on to any necessary retouching.

To the child, however, the painting was finished once he put in the background. The concepts of returning to it "tomorrow" or doing further work on it were really beyond his comprehension at that time.

So I've made two resolutions about patience and the problem of time with my own children, and I strongly urge other parents to do the same:

Resolution #1

Before I thoughtlessly say, "You can do that yourself," I stop to think. I ask myself, do I believe my child really can do it alone? Or am I merely uninterested in her activity at this moment?

Resolution #2

I try to firmly keep in mind that my child's comprehension of time is greatly limited. And I try to avoid such words and phrases as "in a minute," "maybe tonight," "tomorrow," or "in a while." To a small child, these concepts have only a negative meaning. They say, "I'm not going to do it!" If I can't deal with a child's needs at once, I usually try to distract the youngster by offering a positive alternative. For example, if she wants to go outside to play and I still have work to do in the house, I may try to come up with a "game" for her, such as helping me operate the vacuum cleaner.

Being patient and getting in harmony with your child's concept of time aren't easy. But it's essential to acquire these qualities if you hope to develop the kind of confidence that will really help you work effectively with a youngster.

THE CONFIDENCE OF RISK-TAKING

Recently, there was a tragedy in my neighborhood. A young couple gave their small son a tremendous amount of freedom because they didn't want him to develop any phobias. But then, he walked along the edge of an empty swimming pool, fell into the deep end and fractured his skull.

Here, the parents gave their child freedom so that he would develop confidence in risk taking, but they went too far. What did they do wrong? More specifically, what's the distinction between a "foolhardy risk" and "intelligent risk-taking?"

In answering these questions about children and risks, you should take three factors into consideration: 1) the stage of your child's development; 2) The degree of risk involved; and 3) The presence, or lack thereof, of proper equipment to make the risks reasonable.

Here, we're moving into an area that involves more an *art* of dealing with a child, than the laying down of hard-and-fast rules. For example, there is one rather difficult rock climb at a park in the Northeast where the signs warn, "This rock scramble is not advised for children under eight years old."

But still, a friend of mine took his seven-year-old boy on the hike. There were a few tense moments when they had to step out over chasms that dropped 20 to 30 feet down into the cliff. At the end, there was a climb up slanting ladders and precarious rock footholds to a point several hundred feet above the ground.

During this expedition the father, who was accompanying the son, had not quite known what to expect from his youngster or from the particular rock scramble that they had chosen. But once they had completed the course successfully, it seemed that the young boy had grown up in a number of ways almost immediately.

Among other things, the feeling of accomplishment and achievement at having conquered a difficult physical challenge made him more sure of himself with his peers, as well as with his parents. Fortunately, the risk that the father had chosen was just right for this boy's stage of development. By completing the scramble successfully, the youngster experienced a great surge in his own inner assurance.

Of course, if this boy had failed in his attempt to climb to the top, or worse, if he had been injured, his self-confidence might have suffered significantly. For this reason, I believe it's very important for parents to evaluate carefully the risks that are involved and try to be fairly certain that a child can succeed. In this case, the father probably should have 1) taken his son on previous climbs so he really knew the boy's ability, and 2) gone over the course himself first.

At the same time, there are some risks to which I would never expose a very young child. Take the issue of pets such as cats and dogs. As you know, I have my own problems with dogs. But still, I'd say that an animal should *never* be entrusted to a very small child.

Most very young children get excited when they see an animal— *any* animal. And more often than not, they'll run up and try to squeeze and hug it. But if they are too abrupt or squeeze that animal too hard, they're likely to get bitten, scratched or otherwise hurt.

So as far as I'm concerned, a parent should *always* be present when a child is trying to pet a dog or another animal that is not his own. This, I believe, is not a projection of my own fears: rather, it's simple, common sense.

Sometimes, of course, it's necessary just to let a child try something and get a bump or scratch if he fails. Playground equipment provides an everyday example. I've always had a problem with jungle gyms because I'm afraid of heights. So I've found it difficult to keep myself from snapping at my two youngsters, "Watch out! Be careful!"

But I've noticed that when I do yell out this way, I tend to distract them—and those distractions are when slips and falls are most likely to occur. So, even if my heart is in my mouth, I try to allow both Bonnie and Keith some freedom to test their environment and mobility. That's a very important way that they can become more confident about operating in their worlds and at the same time develop their motor skills. Even when I have more serious doubts about a high playground climb or other mildly dangerous venture,

I'll often let them go ahead with it. But I may also provide a kind of parental "net" to catch them or break the fall in case they slip.

After children reach the age of about seven, they begin to understand safety guidelines much better. Sometimes, however, they'll want to test or even break rules, just to express their growing independence. It's at this point that parents must prohibit unreasonable risk taking, and back up those prohibitions with no-nonsense discipline.

In other words, in the early, preschool years, the parents are the ones who choose the risks. Very young children may want to try out their "wings" in a variety of *extremely* dangerous circumstances. But they don't understand what they stand to lose if they fail. So the full responsibility and reigns of control are in the hands of the adult.

After about age six or seven, another variation emerges on the risk-taking issue. The child knows what the rules are, and he may even have a fairly good grasp of what he stands to lose. But preteens and teenagers are still usually not mature enough to exercise good judgment. They may sense there's a serious risk involved in some activity—whether driving at high speed in a car, mountain-climbing without proper supervision or hang gliding. But pressure from peers or the promise of excitement and adventure may overwhelm any feelings of caution inspired by good common sense. In any case, these older youngsters tend to be certain they know best, though often they don't.

So parents must develop an inner assurance about when they should put a curb on risk taking, and when they should allow the child, at whatever age, to fly or fall on his own. And they must keep the courage to step in during these later years and say "no" to unwise teenage activity. Otherwise, risk-taking may get out of hand; the youngster may fail in his attempt to achieve some dangerous, unrealistic goal; and self-confidence, not to mention life and limb, may suffer.

THE CONFIDENCE OF REARING SPECIAL CHILDREN

A new mother approached the hospital crib and looked down at a squirming little object who weighed scarcely more than a loaf of bread, and was gasping for breath. Then, she turned to me and blurted, "How? How will I *ever* be able to care for her!"

This, sadly, is a common reaction on the part of parents whose babies are born handicapped or premature. Parents are disturbed enough when one of these special children is born to them, but things get worse after the youngster has spent weeks or even months in the hospital under the care of specially trained professionals. The mother and father may be frightened out of their wits at the prospect of taking the child home and caring for him on their own.

The mother's self-confidence has usually already been shaken because she's been unable to carry the child to full term or something else has gone wrong during gestation, labor or delivery. So it's not enough to say to the woman, "Your baby is ready to go home now, Mrs. Jones. Aren't you delighted?"

Instead, we medical professionals—including obstetricians, pediatricians and nurses—are learning how to involve parents *from the very beginning* in the care of the tiniest and sickest babies. Certainly, we continue to teach them certain basic physical skills like changing, washing and feeding, but we also help them understand something far more precious and essential to the development of parental self-confidence: We teach them that there is something unique in the very special relationship between them, as parents, and their new child. In fact, their new baby, even though he may be deformed or otherwise handicapped, has something special to offer them and to contribute to their family.

Although I believe firmly that all this is true, I know that it's difficult for many parents to believe it, especially after the shock of realizing they now have one of these special children in their family. Time and again I've encountered a helpless reaction from mothers and fathers, who may even feel that some sort of extraordinary intervention or punishment by God has been visited on their family. Whatever self-confidence they may have enjoyed as expectant parents is now totally shattered.

Even in the worst cases, however, there's still hope if the medical professional is supportive and if the parents are able to get plenty of information about the exact problem their child is suffering from. Knowledge, and the practical strategies that can be based on such knowledge, are effective antidotes to shattered self-confidence. But it's up to the physician and also up to the parents to acquire that knowledge and learn to use it.

On one occasion, I found myself working with parents of a newborn who had a major malformation of the face. "I can certainly understand your shock and grief," I told the mother and father during our first conversation. "But these unhappy events do occur in the natural course of things. They're *not* unnatural!"

After introducing the subject this way, I immediately got more specific with them about exactly what had occurred with their child: "What's happened is that a very normal process of development just didn't finish. For some reason, it got stopped along the way. As in cases of cleft palate or harelip that you've probably seen, there is a point in the development where the tissues don't meet. A genetic signal should have told the developing body to continue until all the parts of the face had joined, but the genes just didn't do their job."

After some further explanations along this line, I then turned to possible ways that plastic surgery and other medical procedures might help to correct their child's appearance. Also, I pointed out the bright side of the birth defect: Even though the youngster's outward appearance was affected, his brain, internal organs and the rest of his body seemed just fine. In other words, we were confronting a cosmetic problem more than anything else.

When these parents finally left the hospital, they were armed with several things that bolstered up their sagging self-confidence. For one thing, they now had *knowledge* about the physical problem faced by their child, and they also understood the medical implications of the problem. Furthermore, they had the beginnings of a *strategy* for dealing with the problem in later years through plastic surgery and psychological counseling. Things always seem much more manageable after we've gained extra information and thought through our responses to a difficult situation.

An absolutely essential factor in strengthening the self-confidence of parents with special children is a sensitive, supportive pediatrician. So if you find yourself in this situation, be sure to pick your doctors carefully. In particular, a sensitive pediatrician, as well as hospital personnel, will encourage parents of special children to:

• *See the child early.* No matter how shocked or disappointed parents may be, the power of the mind to create monsters is far greater than anything nature can accomplish. So you should look that little infant directly in the eye and examine him closely, immediately after birth. That way, you get to know him as an individual; you're less inclined to treat him as some sort of distant, detached tragedy that happened to your family.

• *Touch your special child and be free in showing affection in other ways.* The more mothers and fathers handle their children, no matter what the problems, the more confidence they develop in learning what's expected of them as the caretakers.

• *Be realistic about your child's abilities to achieve.* If you try to measure the progress of a handicapped child against that of a child with more normal abilities, you'll almost always be disappointed. Also, you may very well overlook the fact that your child is, in fact, achieving significant things.

For example, your child may have been born two or three months early, but you may still find yourself during the first year looking for developmental milestones that should occur in the average child. With a premature baby, however, there will inevitably be a lag in development, especially in those early months. So relax! A little more time will be needed in this case to get those muscles moving together and put the coordination in order.

Suppose your child was born two months early, for example. You can't expect her at the age of ten months to be at the same spot in development as her ten-month-old cousin who was born after a full-term pregnancy. Instead, it's more reasonable to think of your child as an eight-month-old, rather than a ten-month-old.

• *Take advantage of frequent trips to your pediatrician.* Again, it's important during the first months and even years at home to continue to gather information about your child's problem and how you can best deal with it. To this end, many doctors, whether they're caring for normal or special children, will reserve a "telephone hour."

This is a time, often scheduled early in the morning, when parents can call in to discuss problems that may not yet have become emergencies. For example, an illness may suddenly strike a child, and parents won't know whether they should bring her in or try to treat the problem themselves. Keeping in touch this way about a child with a handicap can be especially comforting and supportive and do wonders to help parents strengthen their own self-confidence.

THE CONFIDENCE OF UNDERSTANDING EMOTIONAL AND PHYSICAL TIMETABLES

Few things will sap the confidence of a young couple as much as a tendency to worry about how their child is doing in relation to other youngsters about the same age.

"Is he *normal?*" they may ask. Or more specifically, "Is he *on schedule?*

In other words, is he smiling, rolling over, standing, walking or whatever at the time he should be? Is he developing according to healthy timetables for most babies his own age?

Certainly, there are milestones, guideposts and guidelines that indicate in general terms whether a child is moving forward in a normal, healthy way or whether he's running into problems. But it's all too easy to get rigid in interpreting these developmental stages. Many parents even get *competitive* in wanting their child to move ahead at a faster pace than anyone else's.

One thing that particularly disturbs many new parents is their child's emotional reactions at certain stages of development. In particular, adults may have trouble distinguishing between what's truly abnormal and what's just a peculiarity or quirk in their youngster's personality.

To help these parents evaluate their child better, experts like Dr. Stanley I. Greenspan, the head of the Infant Research Unit at the National Institute of Mental Health in Adelphi, Maryland; Harvard's Dr. T. Berry Brazelton; Dr. Joseph Campos of the University of Denver; and others suggest these guidelines for a child's emotional and personal development.

First two months: The child's alertness increases, and he discovers how to calm himself. Typical emotions include surprise, pleasure, disgust and distress. Also, he shows increasing interest in various people and things.

Two to four months: He smiles and looks happily at adults— especially his mother. If he has problems in this stage, he may avert his face from others and act withdrawn. Joy and anger are typical emotions that appear during this period.

Three to ten months: A normal child will play simple "give-and-take" games with his mother and give signals that he likes this interchange. Also, most youngsters will add sadness and fear to their emotional repertoire. Now, the full range of what are known as the "basic emotions" should be present: anger, joy, sadness, disgust, surprise and fear.

Second year: Instead of merely crying when hungry, a normal child will often take his mother's hands and lead her to the refrigerator. Also, he'll begin to display more sophisticated behaviors and emotions. Tender affection will emerge and then shame and pride.

By age six: By age three to four, a capacity for feeling guilty surfaces in most children. Then, by ages five to six, the so-called "social emotions" appear, including humility, confidence, insecurity and envy. This is the time when your child will start developing a solid sense of who he is and what his capacities are—and he'll begin to compare himself to others. Self-confidence, or a lack of it, becomes quite apparent during this period.

Also, it's important to be aware of your youngster's developing intellectual abilities during this phase of life. Her memory will be developing, though it certainly won't mature completely in this phase, so don't expect too much. Typically, it's more natural for an experienced six-year-old to rehearse items that need to be remembered than it is for a three-year-old. On the other hand, if the younger child can be taught to rehearse, he'll tend to remember as much as his older playmate.

Also, a youngster's ability to develop learning strategies and problem-solving abilities improves with age. Young children who have not yet had any schoolwork tend to rely heavily on trial and error in learning new things, and they rarely check their work for mistakes. As they get older, however, they'll learn to become more methodical in their problem-solving abilities and capacity for learning will improve. You, as a parent, can help a child become more systematic and methodical in this process of learning how to learn by making suggestions about more efficient ways of solving problems or learning new techniques.

On the other hand, it's important not to be too controlling or heavy-handed in teaching a child analytical techniques in these early years because a youngster's creativity is also developing rapidly in early childhood and will often reach a peak at about age seven. Dr. Howard E. Gardner, a Harvard psychologist, says that seven-year-olds are often willing "to create new figures of speech, to combine forms and colors in innovative ways, to juxtapose elements that are normally kept assunder." But soon after this age, they become more reluctant to be so creative because their schoolteachers begin to emphasize getting the right answers to questions and doing things in school the "right" way. Such an emphasis on conformity, which is certainly important in building skills, may also suppress creative growth. (*Psychology Today*, May 1987, page 51)

By adolescence: Dealing with confidence, insecurity, envy, shame, pride and other emotions that have emerged in childhood continue to be important. Also, social skills, which youngsters have been developing since their preschool days, increase in importance. Children learn how to behave in school, at church, at parties, in the doctor's office and at different types of restaurants. The social emotions that have emerged by age six become especially important as children interact with one another and find their places among their peers.

By the time they become teenagers, new emotions have arrived, including romantic passion and philosophical brooding. Also, as we've already seen, adolescents develop a deep need to define their own individuality and separate themselves from their parents and families.

Finally, certain qualities and abilities that appeared much earlier, often in the preschool days, may reappear in a more intense form and set the tone for the child's interests and activities in adulthood. For example, as I've noted, a number of researchers have found that certain creative impulses may be suppressed at about age seven when a child gets exposed to the conformity of school. But those tendencies toward creativity may appear again in a more mature form as an adolescent pursues painting, writing or some other creative effort.

These are just general guidelines. So it always helps to talk with your pediatrician and other experts to get a perspective on something you may perceive as a problem. Also, it's useful to watch your child in play and interactions with other children—and to discuss his emotional reactions and physical development with other parents of children about the same age.

If your child's development seems generally in the ballpark of normal growth, then I'd just relax and enjoy him! If you worry needlessly, your own lack of self-confidence is going to be communicated to your child, with unnecessarily negative results.

The "Cranky" Child

But it's not always easy. One particularly sticky emotional problem that confronts a number of parents is that of the "cranky" child. Some babies just cry and fuss more than others, and many new parents worry that something is seriously wrong.

In fact, some of these cranky children may be suffering from a kind of hypersensitivity. In other words, your child may be overly sensitive to light, sound or other outside influences. If this seems to be a problem, be sure to check with your pediatrician.

Sometimes, the youngster may just be going through a temporary phase and some very simple solutions may take care of the problem. For example, a child who becomes irritated by bright light might just be kept in darker rooms. Or one who is bothered by touch might be cradled in a pillow. In any case, many of these problems will tend to lessen and disappear as the child gets older.

Parental reactions in such situations will usually fall into one of three categories, and it may be helpful for you to evaluate yourself to see where you stand:

Reaction #1: The disciplinarian-parent will lean toward punishment because he'll interpret the youngster's crankiness or other unusual actions as "bad."

Reaction #2: The worrier-parent will fuss over the child and become increasingly anxious because they fear the child is ill and they can't figure out what to do about it.

Reaction #3: The third group of parents will get sufficient information to understand what the problem is. Then, they'll accept their baby as normal—or take steps to calm him down.

Obviously, this third reaction is the only one that makes any sense. And it's the only one that reflects the kind of self-confidence that a good parent should have in dealing with a child who is running into a few problems growing up.

If you just stay calm and take certain rational, systematic steps to deal with the problem your child faces, you'll often be surprised at how easy it is to straighten the situation out and restore your own self-confidence. Dr. Terry Brazelton of Harvard, for example, was once actually able to save a woman who was threatening suicide by a rather simple, though penetrating, analysis of her baby's problems.

The woman was beside herself because the child had cried daily for four to six hours over a four-month period. Finally, she phoned the Harvard pediatrician and said she would jump from her 30th-floor apartment unless he gave her an appointment!

During a conversation with the woman, Dr. Brazelton learned that the child was small for his "gestational age." Hence, he was more prone to hypersensitivity than most children.

"I told her that the thing she was doing to calm him down in fact overstimulated him," Dr. Brazelton said, "and that she should do only one thing at a time—like rock him, or sing to him or just hold him."

The day after this consultation, the woman called back and said that the baby had cried for only one hour. By the following week, he was doing just fine.

Here, once again, was a situation in which the solution was rather straightforward and simple. Unfortunately, the parent had completely lost any sense of confidence that she could deal effectively with her child until, finally, she saw no exit from her dilemma other than suicide. Some good, solid advice from a knowledgeable physician restored her self-confidence and her ability to resume her role as the overseer of her child's emotional development.

THE CONFIDENCE OF BEING A FATHER WITHOUT A WIFE

Throughout much of this book, we've focused on the role of the mother, because in our society, it's usually the mother who assumes the role of primary caretaker of children. But actually, single *fathers* have become a growing national phenomenon, their numbers soaring from 225,000 in 1970 to more than 800,000 today. Also, the number of children in these single-father households has increased during that period to more than one million.

In our society, despite the progress we've made in involving men in child-rearing responsibilities, it's not always easy for a man to take on the role of primary caretaker. It's not that men are inherently inadequate in this area! Rather, they just lack experience. When fathers begin to get more accustomed to a certain task, they may do it as well as or better than many mothers—and they often feel quite confident at it.

Some research done by Dr. Geoffrey L. Greif of Widener College in Pennsylvania, indicates that single fathers, as harassed as they often are, can do pretty well at their job. From 65 percent to 87 percent of those surveyed by Dr. Greif felt at ease doing largely unfamiliar household chores like laundry, cooking and cleaning. In addition, more than four out of five of these single fathers were content with their relationships with their children. In short, they experienced significant degrees of self-confidence in the child-rearing role.

But still, Dr. Greif found that many of these single fathers, who had often had their roles thrust upon them by divorce, faced difficulties inherent in the role of single parent. More than three-quarters of them reported difficulty in juggling full-time work and full-time parenting. About one in three had to change their work hours, and nearly the same number were forced to cut down on work-associated travel. As a matter of fact, 10 percent of these working fathers had either quit or been fired from their jobs because of their single-parenting demands.

Other problems are confronted by single fathers.

- It can be difficult to adjust once again to the state of being single—while trying at the same time to raise children. In Dr. Greif's study, single fathers typically had a lot of trouble trying to start up a social life. Also, less than half agreed with the statement, "I feel comfortable being single again."
- The presence of the father's children may reduce the chances of success of any future marriage. Dr. John W. Jacobs of the Montefiore Center in New York reports that 80 percent of the people who get a divorce will remarry, but 50 percent of those remarriages will fail. "And the number one reason they fail is because of the problems of dealing with children from the first marriage," Dr. Jacobs says. (*Psychology Today*, June 1985, page 67)
- At least one study, by Dallas psychologist Richard Warshak and John Santrok, has found that in many cases, children are better

off with single parents of the same sex, rather than of the opposite sex. Specifically, girls being raised by mothers or boys by fathers do better on average on measures of personality and social development.

It's not easy being a father without a wife. But I believe that men *can* successfully carry out this parenting role if they take it seriously and find support from extended family relationships, community organizations and church groups.

One study by Sara Bonkowski, an associate professor of social work at George Williams College in Illinois, has confirmed that single fathers can do as well as single mothers in raising children. In comparing homes run by both divorced fathers and divorced mothers, she found that there was no significant difference between the two groups. Specifically, single fathers *and* single mothers both provided nutritious meals, plenty of physical affection and musical opportunities like piano lessons. In some ways, the fathers even seemed to have an advantage: They made more money and had greater flexibility in their jobs, and as a result they were able to meet many of the needs of their youngsters more expeditiously.

In the last analysis, confidence of a single father will often depend upon how well the man can adjust his personal value system to the demands of child rearing. To put it bluntly, if you, as a single father, continue to feel that your work is the most important thing in your life, you probably won't do too well in your parenting role.

The requirements of being a good parent—and teaching your child in the ways of self-confidence and success in life—can be overwhelming. So in most cases, the single parent must make a conscious decision to put the child's welfare first. Many of the fathers in Dr. Greif's survey discovered this fact in their own experience. And I would expect that you, too, will find that a child-first, family-first set of personal priorities will be essential if you hope to be a successful single parent.

THE CONFIDENCE OF BEING A MOTHER WITHOUT A HUSBAND

Many of the problems faced by single fathers are quite familiar to the single mother. But there are also some differences.

For one thing, there are many more single mothers than single fathers. Dr. Robert S. Weiss, professor of sociology at the University of Massachusetts in Boston, estimates that one out of every six children these days resides in a single-parent home. Moreover, at one time or another in their lives, as many as half of all the children in the United States may live in a one-parent home!

Usually, these single parents are mothers. In his book *Going It Alone: The Family Life and Social Situation of the Single Parent*, Dr. Weiss says that more than nine out of ten of these children live with their mothers.

A major problem that single mothers face is that they tend to become the victims of what's been called ''the feminization of poverty.'' In other words, they are at the low end of the economic scale because, being women, they can't command as high a salary as a man. Also, they don't have a man living at home who can contribute to the family income.

On the other hand, if a woman can solve her economic problems, the prognosis is favorable that she'll be successful in keeping her family together. But if she's recently divorced, she has to move quickly to get her affairs in order because the crucial period tends to be in first year or so after the separation occurs.

Dr. Judith Wallerstein, executive director of the Center for Families in Transition in Corte Madera, California, suggests that single mothers encourage the children in the family—and especially the adolescents—to help out more around the home. She advises that mothers tell their youngsters, ''Look, things are going to have to be different. We're all in this together, and we're going to have to be partners. I'm earning a living for us now. I'm doing it all. So I need your help if this household is going to work.''

Dr. Robert Weiss agrees that this approach ''does seem to foster earlier maturity. Kids are usually proud that they can help and contribute to the family's welfare. They seem self-sufficient, and often that fosters self-esteem. But at the same time, they resent the responsibility and regret not having a carefree childhood.''

A special problem that single mothers have faced is how to raise their sons. Many single mothers worry about their own abilities to usher a young male through childhood, adolescence and into adulthood, especially when the boy grows to a height and breadth where he towers over the mother and is capable of physically picking her up and carrying her around the room.

Yet a study by Ellison Rodgers, a science writer with Johns Hopkins Medical Institutions, and Dr. Michael Cataldo, an associate professor of psychology at Johns Hopkins University, says that Mom can definitely do it! One key, however, in the view of Rodgers and Cataldo is that mothers must stop assuming that the problems their sons face usually result from the lack of a father.

Some special techniques that these authors recommend for rearing a confident son include:

- Negotiation. They say that the boys should be given clear rules to follow, and there should be clear sanctions if those rules are violated. And it's helpful if the rules are arrived at through mutual agreement that results from discussions between the mother and the son. They suggest requiring that pocket money for the boys be dependent upon the child's performance of certain household chores. Or a teenager's use of a car may be linked to the teenager's observing certain rules about getting home at an agreed-upon hour.
- Reliance on other men in the community. Many times, male relatives, friends and other acquaintances will be happy to help a single mother with her son. Of course, the responsibility of an outside adult should usually be limited as to time and place: For example, another father may be willing to take a single mother's son to a ball game on a Saturday or a Cub Scout meeting some evening. Also, single mothers can often arrange trade-offs with male parents. In other words, the single mother might offer to take another child to school if the other child's male parent will spend some time with her youngster.

In any event, it's wise for the single mother to *avoid* rushing into remarriage just to have a man around the house for her male children. More often than not, such motives for marriage may result in the woman's getting the wrong mate, and her sons may be worse off than they were before, when she was single.

For boys or girls, a single-mother childhood can be a double-edged sword for the development of self-confidence. On the one hand, the children may become more independent and self-assured. But there's also the danger that they'll get resentful. The attitude that wins out will depend heavily on the way the mother explains things and whether she relates to the children in a loving way.

Dr. Wallerstein suggests that single mothers keep at least three factors in mind as they're trying to strike the right balance in their households:

1. Don't ask young school-age children to do what they can't do. For example, a six-year-old shouldn't be asked to take care of himself in an empty house or make his own breakfast or lunch.
2. Children should be asked to *share* decision-making on major issues, but the decision-making should *not* be turned over completely to the children. "Parents have to remain parents," Dr. Wallerstein says.
3. Mothers may be able to rely on children as young as nine or ten years old for emotional support. But when they turn to younger children, the burden can be overwhelming for the youngsters.

For example, Dr. Wallerstein notes, discussion of money may frighten very young children. "Some even imagine that this means they will starve," she says.

Even with teenagers, the single mother should be careful. When she relies too heavily on a teen who is already feeling the pressures at home, she may give the youngster a feeling that there's absolutely no strong, reliable adult figure on whom to count.

Clearly, a single mother must be very careful in relying on her children as a source of her own self-confidence. A strong child with a well-developed emotional base may actually be able to become *more* confident by giving Mother advice and nurturance. But if even Mom seems unable to stand on her own two feet, an emotionally shaky youngster may suffer a devastating blow to his own sense of security and self-assurance. So as with many of the other situations we've considered, the single mother must examine closely the precise, individual circumstances in her family before she unloads all her worries and concerns on her offspring.

THE CONFIDENCE OF
BEING A STEPPARENT

Perhaps the most difficult challenge to self-confidence for either a husband or wife is the challenge of being a stepparent.

Various stepparents, in commenting on their position, have the following complaints:

• "You're sort of an intruder."
• "You can't come in in high gear."

- "Stepfamilies don't work like *The Brady Bunch*," adds Elizabeth Einstein, editor of *The Stepfamily Bulletin*—and herself both a stepchild and a stepmother.

Yet stepfamilies are one of the fastest-growing, if not *the* fastest-growing, forms of family life. According to Einstein, every fifth child in the country has at least one stepparent, and in California the ratio is a stepparent for every third child. The number of stepparents, moreover, is growing by more than 500,000 monthly, with more than 15 million individuals now bearing responsibility for children born during their spouse's previous marriages.

One of the major obstacles to harmonious stepfamily living is the child's loyalty to a missing parent, whether divorced or dead. Understandably, many stepparents have a serious lack of confidence in their ability to fulfill their role properly. And this lack of confidence can cause a stepparent to stumble in a number of ways.

For one thing, in their eagerness to make friends with their new family, some spouses fall into the trap of overemphasizing concern for the children.

"Often, stepparents don't realize that the most important relationship that they have is the husband-wife relationship," Dr. Aaron Lipman, professor of sociology at the University of Miami, points out. As a result, a stepparent may neglect the marriage relationship, and this, in turn, may have a negative effect on the stepparent's relationship with a stepchild.

Also, stepparents often take child-rearing problems too personally. They think that everything that goes wrong in the family with the youngsters is their fault because they're the intruders or interlopers. In most cases, of course, this feeling of being at fault is totally unfounded. It's a direct result of the stepparent's lack of confidence in his or her own role in the family. But these fears that may overwhelm a new spouse are very real. And often, some sort of outside help, such as family therapy, will be necessary to put everything back on an even keel.

Fortunately for the bewildered stepparent, much help and advice are available through such organizations as the Stepfamily Association, which has 40 chapters throughout the country. Also, the Family Service Association of America in New York City conducts meetings in various states, with lectures by various authorities on stepparenting.

If you want more information about these two organizations, you might write them at the following addresses:

Stepfamily Association
900 Welch Road
Palo Alto, California   94304

Family Service Association of America
44 East 23rd Street
New York NY 10010

Stepparents who exercise tact, patience and love *can* achieve considerable success in establishing meaningful relationships with their stepchildren. But it's important not to try to supplant the role of a missing, beloved parent. You simply can't expect a youngster to regard you as his real parent when you're not. But if you're realistic, warm and supportive, you'll be much more likely to develop a sure, confident touch in dealing with your stepchildren.

THE CONFIDENCE OF BEING
A TWO-CAREER COUPLE

There are many confidence crises that accompany the two-career family. Today, women comprise more than two-thirds of our work force, and four-fifths of these women will probably become pregnant at some time during their careers. Also, two-career couples are on the rise: For example, their number increased by 800,000 between 1985 and 1986, to a total of 23 million, or 46 percent of all American couples, according to the U.S. Labor Department. By contrast, families in which the husband is the sole worker declined by 700,000, to 23 percent of married couples.

What do these statistics mean for child rearing? For one thing, the number of "latch-key" children, who have both working mothers and fathers and frequently find themselves alone in an empty house, will increase. Also, parents and children will tend to spend less and less time together, a fact that can only bode ill for the future of self-confidence among both children and parents.

In one recent study by the Institute for Social Research at the University of Michigan, the investigators found that working mothers spend an average of only 11 minutes each weekday and 30 minutes per day on weekends in "quality time" with their children. This included activities such as reading to children, talking with them or playing with them. Fathers, most of whom were employed outside the home, spend even less "quality time" with their youngsters: They devoted only 8 minutes to their children each weekday and only 14 minutes a day on weekends! (*Psychology Today*, October 1986, p. 16)

Quality time, involving an intense, one-to-one relationship with the child, is of course extremely important. But there also must be a reasonable *quantity* of this quality time. Clearly, there is *not* much quantity in the average American household if these statistics really do hold up nationwide.

Being a professional myself, I can sympathize with the pressures and problems of a working mother. But still, I go back to a point I made early in this book: If parents want to have children, they must make some tough decisions about how much time and effort they're going to put into that relationship. You simply can't expect to have a significant impact on a child—including a beneficial impact on his self-confidence—if you don't spend any time with him.

On the other hand, various studies show that the children of working mothers can develop as well as the offspring of mothers who don't work. One study by Helen Lerner, an assistant professor of nursing at Lehman College of the City University of New York, focused on middle- to upper-middle-class families, where half the mothers worked and half didn't.

"The similarities between the groups were striking," concluded Lerner. Using standard questionnaires and interviews to determine the impact of child-rearing approaches on child development patterns, she found a fairly equal performance in intellectual skills, the ability to cooperate with others and length of attention span. Her study involved 100 families, with children ranging in age from 30 months to 12 years. About 20 percent of the working mothers kept their children in day-care centers, and the rest used other types of baby-sitting services.

In another study, Felton Earls, a Washington University School of Medicine psychiatrist, asked parents to evaluate 100 preschool children on a standard behavior test. The test focused on such things as child's eating and sleeping habits, moods and fears. Then, after the parents had responded, the researchers called in a team of six psychologists and a psychiatrist to evaluate the same children.

not only be genuine: It will also possess the power to transform your youngster's entire life.

THE ULTIMATE SOURCE OF SELF-CONFIDENCE

The very idea of promoting "self-confidence" may be highly suspect, especially in the opinion of the deep thinkers among us. After all, we are part of what's been called by pop pundits the "Me Generation": We're supposed to be interested primarily in self-fulfillment and self-aggrandizement. In the minds of many people, self-centeredness is what adds up to self-confidence.

But *true* self-confidence goes far deeper than these selfish, egocentric definitions. For most of us, the greatest source of any authentic self-confidence lies in our fundamental philosophy of life. Our ultimate capacities as human beings are tied directly into broader beliefs about the meaning of life.

For most Americans—95 percent of whom believe in God, according to a series of Gallup polls—religious faith has a direct tie-in to self-confidence. If you're firmly convinced that you're a child of God, you'll probably feel limited only by what God can do with you and through you.

For many people, of course, the belief in God only involves a rather superficial intellectual assent to His existence. Religion really doesn't have very much to do with the warp and woof of our daily existence. But the arrival of a child changes all this for many adults.

Children often represent "the catalyst for tremendous growth in adults, especially when it comes to such things as religion" observes psychology professor William V.B. Damon of Clark University in Worcester, Massachusetts. The author of *Social and Personality Development* (W.W. Norton, 1983), Professor Damon says, "Parents must transmit to their offspring what the social order is all about. And to some extent that means parents must first figure out what they believe in."

But children are too smart to buy a half-hearted approach to this question of beliefs and worldviews. Some parents who attend church or synagogue may be "hedging their bets," according to Professor James R. Lundy, author of *A Psychology of Religion.* He notes,

"Some parents are saying, 'Just in case I'm wrong about heaven and hell, my child shouldn't suffer.'"

According to Lundy, too many parents use a "deliver and pickup service"; they merely drop their children off for religious services or instruction. They don't bother to find out whether the particular religious views being promoted actually coincide with their own. Lundy calls this approach "a form of Russian roulette."

Our children deserve better than this, and mothers and fathers know it. Some parents even become aware of the spiritual implications of parenthood as early as the time of birth.

I've worked closely with women who have just gone through difficult labors and have borne babies who must be rushed into intensive care because of life-threatening physical problems. Such women are, in every sense, out of control. They have little influence at that moment over the workings of their own bodies, their feelings or the health of their loved ones.

But I can also think of a number of women who have at least had the seed of faith planted in them before coming into the hospital to give birth. In such cases, a hospital worker who has a similar faith can often sit and talk to the new mother and reinforce her sense that even though she may be out of control for a moment, Someone Else has taken over. Such religious fellowship can restore the new mother's sense that there really is some pervasive order in the world, and eventually, in some way, everything will come out all right.

Later, the patient may not remember a thing that was said to her. But a precious sense of reassurance, the warmth of that fleeting relationship, will remain. That brief support will calm the mother down and give her the security of knowing, "Things are bad, but all that can be done is being done. God is in control, and you just have to trust that He has the power to orchestrate the outcome."

Much the same sort of process occurs when you are dealing with a distraught child who has suffered some deep blow to his self-confidence. Your words may not get through; he may not remember a thing you say. But the feelings of support that you communicate to him—and the fact that you're speaking with authority out of some solid value system—will definitely have an impact. When you touch him, hold him and talk softly but reassuringly to him, you'll let him know that there's really something secure about the world. There's a safe haven where he can rest and regroup his inner forces, even as the outside circumstances seem to be closing in on him.

A powerful personal interaction is taking place here. First, you, the parent, *believe* that what you're saying will work in the child's life. Also, your inner assurance will help the child to believe in you. Finally, the process of emotional healing will take hold in the child, and his self-confidence will blossom once again.

If you're a religious person, it's quite appropriate to tell your youngster at a very early age, perhaps even before he can carry on a conversation, where your ultimate source of comfort and confidence lies. If he hears you promoting your faith and philosophy of life and sees that it works successfully in practice, he'll be more inclined to incorporate it as a part of his own personal makeup.

This is one reason that I advocate giving children religious instruction from an early age. The church or synagogue will reinforce from an outside perspective what's being taught and encouraged at home. In this way, the youngster's ultimate source of self-confidence will extend far beyond himself, to the traditions and doctrines that provide the framework of a living faith.

But it's important for parents *not* to assume that those outside sources of instruction and religious influence are sufficient in themselves. A church or synagogue experience may "take" with some children; but for most, much more is required. Children must actually *see* the faith practiced in the home by the parents if the full impact of a religious worldview is to have any effect.

As I've become more experienced both in my Christian faith and in my profession, I've also gotten much more comfortable about consoling despondent patients. They may ask me, "What makes you think I'm going to be able to cope with this problem? Why do you think there's a way out of this? Do you really believe I can live with this tragedy?"

If they share my faith, I have a ready answer for them. Our faith is our ultimate support. That's why I'm not lying when I tell them that something *can* be done; support *can* be found; we *can* get through this terrifying crisis together.

These days, you hear much talk about the importance of recapturing the old-fashioned doctor-patient relationship. Some experts, like Dr. Herbert Benson of the Harvard Medical School, emphasize that this doctor-patient relationship may often be more important in the healing process than therapy based on drugs or surgery.

Similarly, a warm, supportive, belief-based relationship is essential in the successful rearing of a child. If a child sees that a parent's self-confidence is somehow rooted in an authentic belief system, that child will be much more likely to base his own self-confidence on solid spiritual and philosophical authority. On the other hand, if you try to *impose* self-confidence on your child with quick-fix, superficial types of encouragement—encouragement that is not clearly rooted in what you purport to believe—your child won't be impressed.

Suppose, for example, your child experiences some serious rejection at school, such as failing to make an athletic team or scoring very low marks on some important test. You can always say, "Everything's going to be all right," and leave it at that. But that kind of glib response won't do a thing for your youngster's self-confidence! Instead, it's essential to spend some time with your son or daughter exploring some of the subtleties of the serious challenge or failure that he's just faced. Perhaps you'll have to share some of your own experiences with failure or hardship—and explain how your faith made a difference in those cases.

In any case, an easy answer probably won't go down too well. If your child has been seriously disappointed about something, he'll need continuing reassurances from you, perhaps over a period of days or even longer, to help him get back on a self-confidence track. If he sees that your advice and observations are coming from a firm belief system, he's much more likely to recover more quickly.

As you delve into these deep sources of self-confidence with your child, you may well find that your own personal faith and belief systems are undergoing a change. At first, you may be disturbed because you don't have all the answers. But eventually, as you wrestle with these issues, you'll probably be strengthened as well.

10

Your Self-Confident Child

Self-confidence, when properly understood, is quite a broad concept. This important inner quality combines our own sense of security and self-worth with the great questions of who we are and what the fundamental meaning of life really is. As such, self-confidence becomes an ultimate key to happiness and satisfaction in life.

Self-confidence may also lead to success in the narrow sense of achieving fame, fortune or high career goals. Certainly, some of the greatest achievers have been people who truly believed in themselves and in their ability to accomplish great things in life. But a sense of inner assurance will take us much further than that, as we gain greater confidence in relating to others and in setting our priorities in life.

But remember, as you focus on *your* youngster, it all begins in early childhood. It's most helpful to think of the development of self-confidence in terms of a series of building blocks, which begin at birth and move steadily onward, through toddlerhood, the preschool years, the early school experience, adolescence and finally in adulthood. In this book, I've emphasized the early years, from birth to about age seven, because most of the studies, as well as my own experience, indicate that these are the crucial times when the main foundations of later self-confidence are laid. Of course, as we've seen, there are plenty of issues and crises relating to self-confidence that confront adolescents and their parents. But in most cases, these challenges can be met and dealt with successfully if parents have helped their children establish a solid core of self-confidence in early childhood.

But in these final words, I'd like to emphasize that the essence of self-confidence is not primarily a self-centered focus on the individual child. It's too easy, when we refer to self-confidence, to assume that we're saying, in effect, "You have to realize you're a strong person! You're really somebody! You're important!"

Certainly, some people need to shore up their self-esteem, especially if they've been beaten down by oppressive, negative parents or others in positions of authority or influence over them. But in the final analysis, true self-confidence doesn't involve this sort of self-aggrandizement.

Instead, the self-confidence that we've been talking about in the previous pages encompasses a building up of the individual's self-image *in the context of* relationships with other people. It doesn't do a bit of good to be self-confident if you can't operate effectively with others.

Almost all success and satisfaction in life have something to do with some other person or groups of people. The truly self-confident person gets along well with family members, colleagues at work, fellow believers in religious groups and coworkers in volunteer organizations. The Lone Ranger may have been self-confident, but remember: He always had Tonto at his side!

Self-confidence, then, is not just a sense of assurance about what your child can do individually, in some sort of cultural or social vacuum. Rather, genuine self-confidence is a firm, unshakable reference point that will allow your youngster to know, with a sense of joy and clarity, that he's capable of operating effectively and meaningfully among other human beings. And with this strength, he'll be in a position to act as a standard-bearer of ultimate values and beliefs that can change the world for the better.

Index